Constellation

Cloudbank Books
Corvallis, Oregon

Constellation

H. L. Hix

Printed in the United States of America

FIRST EDITION

ISBN: 978-0-9849991-3-2

The cover image: *Saturn's Hexagon,* silk and synthetic
fabrics; fused and sewn applique; 79.5"h x 68.5"w; 2018.
It appears here by kind permission of the artist, Petra Soesemann.
The author photo is by Kate Northrop.

1 2 3 4 5 6 7 8 9 0

Cloudbank Books
216 SW Madison Ave.
Corvallis, OR 97333
www.cloudbankbooks.com

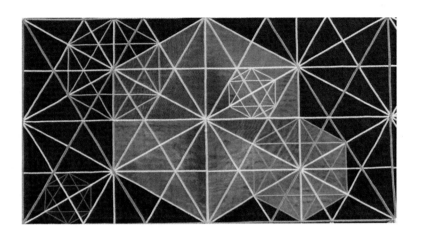

Contents

Luminosities

First principle: suffer no first principles. First labor: mark
what eludes. First loss: landscape, from butterfly-delectated
and bloomlorn down to undone. First futility: test focus
against scale. Small, precise; precise, precious; precious, prescient. Not
in itself but for what, in other conditions, with senses
trained to and by it, I might perceive radiating from it.
Against landscape, butterfly. Scolding its intemperate wings,
strict pattern. Within that pattern any moment of color,
behind that moment one grain of dust. There's a *reason* we bow
to brilliance: coruscations escaping a caught trout's bright scales,
ultramortality of meteor meeting atmosphere.
That dust: seeing *it,* do I see exactitude made essence?
Light bent to cobalt? A concentration of concentration?
Whole in one grain, whole in all, luminosity holds secret
some larger than itself that no other than itself could tell.

Tell me where my name came from, name what worlds it roamed, what orbits
it escaped, before it broke apart against strict atmosphere,
mixed its dust, itself as dust, with this our dust. Say what ur-dust
collated colors, mattered them into patterns. I don't mind
that it's dust, if it glints. Every day I mind a little less
that myself am dust. Every day I *am* dust a little more.
One meteor I knew fell hard, ladder to studio floor,
not far, just time to rename himself before he broke apart.
Not my plan. No ladders in my studio, and I won't *need*

to break apart if I keep breaking up the way I have been.
That last-thing renaming, though, I envy him. If I *did* fall,
would gravity break me apart, or would my own body weight?
I'm breaking up now so fast, maybe I *am* breaking apart.
Dust-dense, dust-lustrous, doesn't mean I can *choose* to coruscate,
or what atmosphere will falsify my flight, rename it fall.

This fall, a second labor to neighbor the first: liberate
from leaf-litter some eaten-to-pattern fallen. Part-eaten.
I don't pretend to translate such messages, but *do* pretend
they *are* messages. To some attunement other than myself,
but a message is a message. Legible or not, a script,
any script, is precise, and precision, any precision,
precious. It is of math what mesmerizes us: so precise,
and *everywhere*. In that leaf's outline, math. In its symmetry,
the similarity of its veins' branching to limbs' branching,
those very limbs through which it fell. The ratio of the measure
of one mouth to radii curved into the pattern that mouth
cursived through the leaf. Math everywhere, messages everywhere:
in the leaf's having lilted down, in the ultraleveling
of those symmetrical inevitabilities, its fall
and mine. In my leaflikeness, rustle for rustle, hush for hush.

Hush, son. Just hush. I lost whole lives taking for first principle
this, offered as one. Offered early and often. Less often,
though, than I was told to toughen up. Told *toughen up,* then shooed
ruinward. Serried stained-glass stories turned sun-stunning gust-stirred

sediment. Scuff-dust of coruscations past, those meteors
all broken apart, garnished, sure, with trees and luminous birds,
trestles and fossils and paper cups, but ultimately silt,
as (here on this meteor-marked, meteor-measured surface)
which of us is not? Glory be to God for scaffolded things,
all things mortared, architectural, square, planed, but don't pretend
they'll last. *Yes, Socrates, Simmias and I do share the fear*
our souls will scatter in the first good gust, dispersed as surely
as these our dust-bodies. As surely, as widely, as swiftly.
Turns out toughness tightly tracks the tendency to break apart.
Many right-angled things; not many *keep* angles right for long.

I long (as of us who does not) for principle and pattern,
the ultraordinality of trestle trestle trestle,
equivalence of measured and measuring, kept promises
of level and parallel, of gentle long-radiused curves,
something shiny and silent to run beside for what distance
I still can run, each day a little less. Shiny, and silent
except when they sing. I've longéd long for luminosity,
but I don't mind that those trestle-trued parallels more often
offer up rust. We don't get to *choose* whether we oxidize.
No ladder in my studio, but at my desk I digest
harde yron, one spike, rust-crusted, that rust-dusted my palm the day
it unbalanced me for half my morning run. Mon semblable,
mon frère, twin cast-off, competitor for ferroused of them all.
Daily, just before I begin brocading my breaking up
I nod to its red-blessed right angles, that rust rounding them off.

Often, waiting at the crossing, I count coal cars as they pass.
Always those rail cars (… 89 … 90 …), never the flashings
of worry lights lining the warped, striped arm that blocks the two-lane.
I keep odd hours, this town is small, but still behind me traffic
backs up. Lowered, the warning arm halts just off horizontal;
raised, it veers just off vertical. My father passed on to me
his stoop, his father's stoop, so I'm not quite vertical myself.
Horizontal soon, though. Level, parallel to those trestles,
trued by removal from lights flashing and traffic backing up.
Yesterday, malfunction left the arms down, passing train or no,
so two boys parked their pickups and lifted the arms, lights flashing,
to let us stuck cars cross. This town is small: our boys pack pistols,
but take politeness as a point of pride. *Yes, ma'am.* And patience.
Maybe not a bad translation of the larger than itself,
maybe as precise a measure as these my keepings count.

I count all the time. Steps down the aisle to my seat in the plane,
steep steps up one spire of Sagrada Familia. It's a thing.
Number of carts corralled in the parking lot at the market,
eyelets paralleled up each pair of shoes in the waiting room.
DSM labels us OCD. You know us, we who count,
to whom ultracardinality prototypes all pattern.
Numbers are *everywhere,* luminous convergences of sign
with referent. In my ladderless studio, for instance:
number of mugs turned penstands, number of pens upright in each;
number of sips of coffee permitted, number of minutes
enforced between sips. Sometimes one number keeps for its secret

some other: my body weight conceals how many long winters
before I break apart, or more likely how many short nights.
In number the larger than itself proves larger than itself,
leaves messages: leaf veins, those scales on that coruscating trout.

Tryouts never worked for me. Long before I'd matured enough
to fail at what might matter, fail in ways that damage others,
I was better at counting trestles and collecting fossils
than at completing out routes, posting up, or stealing second.
Even then I sensed that any ladder I could climb would need
to be thrown down once climbed; that any life that shared life with me
would not be life, or shared; that the larger than itself never
revealed itself *in* the world or *as* itself. Hushed, it let on
only *that* it was, not *what*. Which left me friend-thin, but offered
consolations: gravel (fine in the drive, coarse between trestles)
held fossils, slim conical shells no bigger than the body
of a butterfly that, smaller than me, more hushed and less there,
hints how much larger than itself is the larger than itself.
Sometimes (instead of cones) clustered semicircles that in life
must have stacked, but for stillness spilled, little heaps of letter c.

I see trains less often than I hear them. From here I can't count
the coal cars, quite, but the railyard's not far, a few ladder-lengths,
so I *can* count each day how few trains trestle past. I hear them
and feel them, that's how huge they are, how much they carry, how much
they weigh. When I say they *rumble* by I mean they reunite
incus and malleus not only with their cousins talus

and calcaneus but also with their elsewise forgotten
elsewise kin, those gravel-patterning fossils, spiraling out
their ultrafractality, fibonacciing their golden
(and God knows what other luminous) ratios, recalling
renaissances past, and past them, origins more ultimate.
But it's not my skeleton I fret for as I break apart.
Think how much soft tissue they imply, all those perfect spirals,
how perfectly absent all softness proves. Think how *long* absent,
how dust-destined, whether or not it sang for its one second.

Second principle: that turning turns out platonic solids
does not entail that toughening trues the toughened. I *have* tried,
first toughening up, later truing. Tried both, managed neither.
Told they kept together, I thought earning either would win both.
But wherever it's been promised me I'll find identity
I've stumbled instead into elsehow, otherladen. Promised
parallels prove perpendiculars: it's a pattern, a thing.
No matter how fast they cardinal past, I can count the cars;
go how slow they will, I can't read their graffiti. Don't pretend
to comprehend even what I recognize as messages.
It's a thing about messages, a pattern: don't need to read
what they spell out, to mark what they don't. That shell-freckled gravel
where I grew up, I thought *it* couldn't keep a secret until
I saw the sandstone here, meteorfish not schooled *in* numbers
but *as* number, not rust but rust-colored, soft tissue and all.

All the falls that have followed that preliminary stumble,

that first time my ankle (for no good reason, with no warning)
gave out, reinforce that, be how brief it may, the interval
first fall to final will call forth from me plenty more mistakes.
I can't count yet how many times I *will* fail, and I've lost count
of the times I've failed before. That first fall barely barked my knee
but I see what it portends. The pattern's plenty legible,
regular as fine ribs, fixed rows strict across those fossil fish.
I'm no Leibniz concocting a calculus, but I can count.
There goes one more coal train, here's another fossil skeleton.
The night sky here shines, no whit less luminous than the daytime.
Darker, sure, but meteors to count, constellations to name,
coruscating planets, a moon often larger than itself.
Of the riots in my childhood, I understood nothing, knew
nothing to fear larger than my father's being gone all night.

Night, less riotous once my father's goneness got secured, now
hosts less to fear. We don't get to *choose* whose absence our bodies,
so surely breaking up, attest to. I can't count the fathers
and the fathers of fathers whose always already listing
my stoop stores up: how many now horizontal skeletons,
attesting to how much soft tissue, how swiftly gust-dispersed.
It's a lot of learning from the last in line to hush, a lot
of teaching the next. I stand last in line, got no next to teach.
For whom am I demonstrating how to take it on the chin?
I absorbed the importance of reporting on the riots,
but I didn't catch to whom it was important to report.
Still, darkness looms large here, larger than itself, more luminous,

meteor-freckled, more platonic than solid. *Such as this,*
Meno: shape is what limits a solid. Limits it in space.
Of its limits in time I am myself the very measure.

Measure up: another principle pressed upon me, deformed
from all that passing down father to son along that long line,
the line that ends in me, that (as they might say) survives in me
or that (as I myself might say it) I survived (a dispute
not worth settling, so briefly could either position hold true).
Think how many ways my life now out-easies their hard lives when.
No land line, for instance, so the call that outlines my ruin
will not wake me. Let even the inevitable listen
first to my left message before leaving its message for me.
To undertake is to deform this third labor: outlisten
listening. Hear what can be heard only by not being heard:
the moment when slow drizzle, inaudible in its falling
but tapping, gathered into gutters, and hissing, whisked off leaves,
turns to snow. No sound, that's the task: to overlisten, to hear
as hush *and* message the nothing more hush, nothing less message.

Message the First. Overheard. The never to be fossilized
ever turning, of itself, to snow. It vanishes, but not
into green undergrowth. It collapses, not without drawdowns
in drowned towns downstream. It drains, but not into the reservoir.
It stains, though never the location of the leak. It buckles,
not from flawed construction but from flawed calculation. It splits,
but not along a preexisting fault. It tears easily,

but not along the perforation. It condenses, and not
without rotting the sill. It shatters, but not because some voice
asserted too much too high-pitched beauty. It evaporates,
but not into clouds to relieve some drier place. It splinters,
less the effect of lightning or of an ax than as their cause.
It spills, then seeps between warped floorboards and soaks into the joists.
It levers logic, gristles grammar. It only *seems* dormant.
It stops rising, though not by the previous high water mark.

Mark the cave walls. What if first principles stint not principles
but impulses? If insight more often follows accident
than principle? My ashblacked palm against the limewhite cave stone
to steady me as I stand proves the handprint that pries one self
from its other, one species from the rest. Fire recommits all
to the elementary. Gesture layers elemented
onto elemental, perplexing pattern into shape, shape
into figure. Makes of us makers, we who see that we see,
we who see ourselves seeing. We who fess our featherlessness.
Now, Theatetus, imagine your soul an aviary.
I don't miss the wings we never managed, so much as I miss
those nictitating membranes we misplaced. Poor substitutes, these,
my semilunar folds. Not much help even against cold wind,
never mind sand or water, never mind snow-doubled sunglare.
It's not just parts of me that are vestigial, though: it's the whole.

My whole history a summing of vestigialities,
my whole person the sum. Because neither whole reduces to,

either is emblematized by, any of its parts. That pause
at the crossing, say, counting coal cars. Not by the crossing itself,
its tense mistrust between ir- and ultra-regularity,
right-angled turns and best keep curves gradual, gradients low;
not by the cars, extend how far they will in both directions,
impose how suffocatingly they may the horizon line.
Not by my counting per se, its substitution of number
for numbered, internal pattern for external patterning;
but by the pause, its twisting of distance into duration,
of what extends beyond conscious thought into what outlasts it.
Glory be to God for scattered things, all things rusted, crusted
who knows how, constellating fossiled, piled, rail-governed gravel:
nails and keys and halves of hinges, halves of hasps and such what-not.

Not that I know what everything *is* that I find abandoned
to railbed gravel. Bent spike, sure, *that* I can identify,
but not, say, this just-as-rusted just-as-iron J, a hook,
a question mark, channeled and notched. Must have helped hitch car to car,
though helped exactly how, who knows. It's heavy enough itself
to have borne whatever weight trailed behind it, all those coal cars,
all that coal from all those holes perforating Powder River.
Coal cars lend themselves to counting; not so the coal they carry.
It's how we assign stable value: by saying how many
when we mean how much. As I do now, here, thus. It matters, though,
what we count and what we don't, what we count and how we count it.
Less because some of us do, but more of us don't, distinguish
right from wrong, true from false, than because as certain countings test

how much against how many, their counters conform how many
to how much. How much more frequently we perform the latter.

The ladder I don't keep here in my studio wouldn't fit,
either, in the shed. My house, smaller than most in this small town,
and older, recounts a displaced past when neighbors shared ladders
and left them outside. No three-car garages, not here, not then.
They let their ladders show through snow, loaned them one neighbor to next,
leaned them against patched pasteboard siding, as I would lean mine now,
had I a ladder to lean, had I one to lay across ice
for rescue. There's a second futility: do anyway
what you would have done had you arrived in time, known what to do.
Had there *been,* even then, anything to do. Turns out *rescue*
more often means *retrieve the body* than *restore to safety.*
A fact about outer lives that says what about our inner?
Not that (in a town so dust-dressed, pond-destitute) many drowned,
but when one kid did, at whose woodstove was the rescuer warmed,
by whom was the ladder returned, leaned against whose peeling paint?

Pained means nothing, least of all knowing. After experience
knowledge, like rescue, occurs too late, performs its own failure.
He must, so to speak, discard the ladder after climbing it.
This small town surely taught then, as it still teaches now, to say
nothing, *how* to say nothing, just so, to the grief-stiff parents
next week at the hardware store. It's not the nothing that is said
that so fear-festers the nothing-sayer. Not the nothing said,
but the necessity of saying it. Not the nothing said,

but that the roles of sayer and said-to might have been reversed,
might be, and soon. *Will* be. Not the nothing said, but the *having*
nothing to say, not now, knowing oneself naught-nudged, knuckled from
one inevitability to its identical next.
We don't get to *choose* which fragile surface we fall through, into
which altered light. We don't get to choose which pattern we follow,
choose when what must happen happens to us, or how suddenly.

Suddenly, though, is what my constant counting tries to avert.
Ultracardinality excludes surprise. Number insists
event imprints pattern, swears pattern realizes sequence.
In all those stories all those stoop-vectors in the line I end
demanded that each next accept as true, the Storyteller
counts and counts, confessing each story sequence-haunted, number
its dream and nightmare. *Then appeared as portent a red dragon,*
seven heads, ten horns, on each head one diadem. Here I pledge
to make your heirs numerous as sand grained under grinding sea.
Not one sparrow falls, not one hair grows on your head, uncounted.
That sparrow calculus, substitution of number for care,
makes it haunting, too, not merely startling, each time some sparrow,
always *suddenly,* stuns itself against the god-timbred glass
of my ladderless studio's one window. *They* don't all fall,
those redirected sparrows, but their each crash foretells that *I* will.

Will and testament, my last, let this stand in place of, serve as.
Something has to, soon, so many have the moments now become,
so long now do they last, of syncope. Simply to stand up

after I've been seated brings it on. It's not dizziness, quite:
more a fading out, the world fading from me, me from the world.
I don't often faint, but I've learned to rise slowly, in stages:
uncross my legs, pause; feet to the floor, pause; straighten my back, pause.
It helps if I can steady myself, one hand against a wall.
Everything goes grainy, gray. All else recedes, so I recede.
My urge is not at my ultimate recession to transfer
what things I own to my less swiftly receding beloved,
but before then — *now* — to consign what cannot at all be owned
to whom it may concern. Not the squirrel balance-beaming across
the half-inch-wide fence-post tops, but the snow so to-and-fro-fraught.
Not the snow, but how this its second falling favors its first.

First things first, though. Or (the point) *before* the first. Antecedents,
preliminaries. *That's* what my ceaseless counting rehearses,
what all this ultranominality seeks: what conditions
the conditions I experience, what makes the possible
possible. My one-windowed studio, by measuring out
my life in sparrow-thumps, poses as sole salience this test:
against what background discern, by what means reckon, how address
oneself to, the larger than itself? I count because I don't
believe in sum, because sequence exceeds sum, because I seek
access to that excess. Which my compiling percepts won't grant,
but here's one: one string of white holiday lights not strung along
but heaped atop one torso-tall bookshelf, reiterated
in framed glass that secures a semblance more fragile than glass itself.
Heaped in smaller numbers than stars that stipple-still my small-town sky;

still, similar susceptibility to constellation.

Constellations: patterns found or imposed? Patterns, or pattern?
Does it matter more that what light now alerts me to Alkaid
left its birthplace 147 years before
the light I know now as Megrez, or that, except for Dubhe
and Alkaid, the Dipper's points pull each other, drift together?
That they drift thus together, or that they are drifting apart?
That Alkaid burns twice as far as Dubhe from our wanderer,
or that when I see them I see them next to one another?
Flank, thigh, base of the tail, black horse, navel. *What then have we learned,*
Simmias, if not that to know we must escape the body,
discerning with only our souls what only soul can discern?
What have I learned if not that under stars that spend hydrogen,
I myself, here in my ladderless studio, am dust, spent?
If not that their drifting apart, begun before I began,
will persist long after my briefly-gathered dust grains disperse?

Dispersals mark precipitous transitions, one principle
of order yielding to some other, the ordered now ordered
into what the reordered may not recognize as order.
This at whatever scale, vast to minuscule, without regard.
Our universe, once softball-sized, then dispersed, still dispersing.
Those rioters I was too young to understand, much less join.
Embers in the woodstove. Schooled meteors, schooled meteorfish.
This dust so briefly body, so tenuously *my* body.
New order from old, old principle to new, each transition

solicits its own close observation, careful listening.
Only when I run along the tracks do I witness the train
swirl the snow back up from its rest among the trestles, back up
higher than my head, higher than the tops of those tall coal cars,
then watch the snow (even, once the train has trestled so far past,
hear it) reiterate its first falling, this time through sunlight.

Some light from without, some from within. Some without light, some with.
Knowing so helps how? Doesn't suss trestle-steady from gustlorn.
Doesn't get me from the strict shadow of the crossing signal
crossing coal cars' ribs far faster than I can count the ribs crossed
to interiority unlimited by history,
the condition all those stoop-cues whose posture I replicate
were more sure of than clear about, to which they fixed such tags as
the substance of things hoped for, the evidence of things not seen.
Who thought themselves inclined toward what I find myself stooped by.
Those coal trains enforce limits from history thunderously.
Run along the tracks, though, in the direction opposite them
and near enough to touch each ribbed car as all thrum past: you feel
the earth beneath your feet unsolided *and* feel each least click
against your glasses as those kicked-up snow crystals imitate
at N-gauge the sparrows testing my studio windowpane.

Pain that asserts is asserted by my bodily decay,
the way leaks that expand are expanded by the craquelure
discomfiting the concrete that feigns foundation for my house.
Craze twice, crumble once. Ice-split, water-worn: either way undone.

Scumbled surface, humbled structure. One finality or two,
the all-too-swift (veering toward you across the median)
and this, the all-too-sure? Is the Structure unsound, or too sound?
Is too sound *possible*? How would too sound differ from unsound?
How would two sounds differ from one sound? Does this loss, the second,
of definition, negate the first or compound it? Mist, fog,
that trainblown snow, create not quite complete light, not quite whiteout.
That I'll not soon forget: caught crossing the pass, blizzard-blinded.
I couldn't see the hood of my own car. Lose the slowed, snow-slurred
red eyes I followed, and *I* was lost. Fear that complete, I learned,
tenders of the emptier-than-itself one intimation.

One intimacy compounds another. That blizzard's blurring
of figure substituted, for landscape lumpy with things lit,
light itself, as its muting of trucktrundle created me
listener to the listened for. I'm used to finding quiet,
not to finding myself found by it. I'm used to findings-out,
for most of which even my honesty, howgauntsoever,
stands honesty enough. That whiteout, though, proved a finding-in,
erasure of figure as final figure, overfigure,
familiar figures (desire, inspiration) figured over,
antefigure of the dream in which a scrim of dragonflies
(skydivers converging during freefall) organizes as
pyramid, mosquito net, cranberry-tinted baldachin
hung from the stiller-than-itself, covering the quieter-.
Those wings, already transparent, erased by motion, erased
all noise with their hum, erasure not by more noise but by less.

Less noise than that dreamed dragonfly tent, that light-level whiteout,
what? What if not this rust replacing these railroad spikes I keep
in a coffee cup (round, upon my desk)? Their ferrousness makes
my sparrow-fretted, ladderless studio surround that cup.
One spike enforces limits from history less clumsily
than the coal cars that, until I limped it home, had been swirling
snow over it long before that long line of stooped silhouettes
stopped at me. The spike still reads, in block caps, WMC.
(FDR, Executive Order 9139:
the War Manpower Commission shall establish policies
governing Federal programs relating to the recruitment,
vocational training, and placement of workers to meet
the needs of industry and agriculture.) Like this spike, I,
by-product of those needs, bear their imprint. We don't get to *choose*
what parallels rail past us, what trestles we testify to.

I testify not to some secret but to all secrecy.
One crescent of snow frozen to the front of each tanker car.
I reason to wholeness from practice of partiality.
Each crescent of snow, eyebrow to each tanker car's one cold eye.
These fragments find in fragmentation my sole integrity.
Those cars compose graffitied sentences, their syntax secret.
I testify not to secrets but to secrecy itself.
A row of rusting oil drums, one letter spray-painted on each.
I reason toward wholeness but practice partiality.
All caps, those sprayed-on letters: W-A-S-T-E-D.
These fragments follow fragmentation, precede integrity.

The silver spray paint protests its own fading into that rust.
I testify not in secret but by means of secrecy.
I reason to wholeness by practicing partiality.
These fragments profess fragmentation my sole integrity.

Integrals integrate infinitesimals, into which
category can be placed, once compared to the larger than
itself, paneblind sparrows, bamboo ladders with lashed-on rungs,
conical fossil shells still secret inside gravel cobbles,
hasp halves, hinge halves, other such rusting what-nots, all things blown down,
grown over, who knows when, not to mention whiteout-frightened me.
Thus *this* integral, this delivering-over of myself
to this fourth labor, imposed by the larger-than-itselfness
of the larger than itself, before which we rest are become
infinitesimals. Not by story, sequencing each next
after its previous, finding out for my half-orphaned friend
her furtive father, will I entice my farther closer.
My labor, not to tell all but to list each, not as story
but instead of story. My life as sorites: this hasp half,
this strict meteorfish, this otterlorn lozenge of sea glass…

I see glass when I should see through it. I see the smoke alarm's
green ceiling-star supervising my insomnia. I see
a ladder lain across the gap between one tarpaper plane
and its puddle-pocked next (inviting crossing, portending fall)
when I should be scission-busy gridding my own commitments.
I see myself seeing when I should see what my seeing sees.

I hear those coal-burdened trains baritone their ad baculum,
drowning me out, despotic as Job's cloudgod shouting him down.
Nights in my studio I hear mice rile the walls and crawlspace,
raccoons accost the compost, *something* stalk across the shingles.
Not to mention hearing in my head voices of long-dead friends,
the way I see floaters in my eyes. I feel against my chest
as fading warmth the hot-water bottle I tuck between
T-shirt and sweatshirt. I hear my own voice, counting not to sum
but to measure, counting out not *one two three* but *one one one.*

One prior to, one alongside, one beneath. One written in
a familiar hand and with familiar characters, but in
unfamiliar grammar with an unfamiliar lexicon,
to be read but not by me. *Then do you agree, Protarchus,*
that the soul resembles a book, onto the pages of which
memories and perceptions write? Or resembles a backward
university town on the shop-window-shard-stricken streets
of which memories and perceptions riot? While some small boy
in mismatched, passed-down flannel pjs under grandma-patchwork
in the two-bedroom tumbledown his parents rent wonders why
his mother's crying, why his father isn't home yet from work.
Unaware that otherwhere (near enough to count for next door)
some other child (one one one) understands as little about
why her father has not come home for months, never will again.
Or a wind-downed tree no memory or perception can right?

Write the truth. Right. As soon as I finish scribbling these my fears.

If this *referred,* if I were out to right the relationship
between word and world, I'd be moonblued now, out in the railyard,
not surveilled by the desklamp-chiaroscuroed second self
in the sparrowlorn studio window corroborating
my insubstantiality. No use for this nice paper,
nice pen. I'd be skulking, McMurphy-ski-capped, between coal cars,
clutching cans to spray-paint not these many words but the one word
that, itself, graffitied in letters taller than I am tall,
would right Anaximenes: *No least particle is the least,*
no greatest whole the greatest. Each defers to the never not,
the more than equal, larger than itself, smaller than itself.
I'd know just where someone before me had bent back the chain link
to shinny through, I'd shush each step across the fossiled gravel.
I wouldn't mind the elements: the windier the better.

Better to say *I'm suffering* than *This landscape is ugly.*
Easy to draw a landscape, more difficult to possess one.
Emotions shape the landscape of our mental and social lives.
New outer landscape, sanction to renew my inner landscape.
Landscape, setting for the stream-laundered, line-dried, sun-faded self.
No practice of practice without a theory of practice.
Better to say *I'm not myself* than *This landscape is nowhere.*
My challenge to provisionality is provisional.
Absences shape the landscape of our mental and social lives.
It's just a sequence of locations, not a trajectory.
Landscape alerts me to my cloud-compacted, cloud-confined self.
What map does not, at all its edges, blur into conjecture?

Better to be lost inside myself than lost to this landscape.
Emotions litter the landscape of my spiritual life.
Landscape registers rivered other with cottonwooded self.

Self-definition, though, does not look at desire, the body,
lost youth, lost love, like I look at this trestle-stapled landscape.
Does not contest, but reifies, revisionist mythmaking.
It is not this, Critias, that worries me, whether, knowing
what knows itself, I would know myself [reflexivity, check;
transitivity, check], *but how to distinguish what I know*
from what I don't. Here's a third futility: find the quiet
in which to find the quiet-found. In which to find this quiet,
self-defined mayfly, motionless on this light-wet windowsill,
its whole body smaller than the pin portion of a push-pin,
its wings so sheer they show up only as shape, not as substance,
only as trace, not as texture, only as the idea,
not as the business, of flight. This mayfly, quiet-complete,
at least as absent as it is present, this mayfly than which
in this swift world I exist by what trice longer, what whit more?

More than you would find in an hour out and back along the tracks
would be one answer to who posted the perplect *How many*
railroad spikes do I need to drive into my head to become
a true Christian that is against evolution? One answer,
though, might prove not enough. Not nearly. Might need a whole passel.
Passels, plural. Trestles, fossils, pestles, spikes. Pistols. Phone calls.
Answers might outschool meteorfish in our star-pebbled sky.

Might be why fundamentals prove hard to find, hard to figure.
Why degree is shak'd, which is the ladder of all high designs.
Might be, too, why what most *is* might least *look like* a love poem.
Why *this* love poem looks so like what looks little like itself,
why it looks so little like what it looks after, looks toward.
Why, crossing the footbridge over the railyard, I go dizzy
when a train seisms below, perpendicular to my path,
pupil *and* perpetrant of the more northerly than itself.

The more than itself I sing, no simple separate person.
No person at all. More a ruckus, hoedown, hullabaloo.
I don't affect to be a spoken-through, though I do protest
I am spoken *around.* Numberless as fossils in gravel,
those voices. Various as butterflies freckling a landscape.
Audible exactly as those butterflies are visible.
The neotropical genus *Heliconius* contains
numerous polytypical species with marked color
differentiation controlled by a small number of genes
and maintained by ultrastabilizing selection pressures
in each mimetic environment. Head and eyes very large
for its body size. Pupae and larvae are cryptic, and spurred.
Tiny acraea, orange acraea, postman, blue Grecian,
zebra longwing, five-spotted longwing, hermathena longwing,
tiger heliconian. Glasswing, shown here in flight and at rest.

Addressed to what it cannot address, tested against what tests
but is not tested: only *this,* by my choice? or *all* I do,

necessarily? It's lost just like the rest, like she is lost,
that first cry to foster celeste and the sister made our first
by the fostering, though since that once we've sung no else than what
she sang. My calendar insists it's spring; this weather, winter.
Give over, give up, give in, give way. Please forward. Postage due.
For me to tell you how I feel, you'd have to care more, not think
you know already, plus this: I'd need to know better myself.
Put those back, son, they don't belong to you. Try to guess which hand.
Yesterday was colder, snowy, but today's *much* windier.
She can't see what's happening to her. Circumstances have changed.
If you'd told me sooner, I could have changed my flight. No swimming.
No trespassing. No soliciting. No rest for the weary.
That didn't take long. Can you help me? There's something in my eye.

I am not dead, but I am not. There are things I can't tell you
because others are involved. And things I can't tell you, because.
I contradict my own principle of non-contradiction.
The creek often freezes over, but never freezes solid.
I mean to tell you more than I can say. These found fossils *say*
only skeleton and chitin, but still tell of soft tissue.
I am dead less as the crow flies than as the creek meanders.
Clear nights I see stars speckle the creek; dark nights, guess what I hear.
The less *my own* my contradictions are, the more principled.
Who before this snow knew how black the creek was, or how crooked?
I'm telling you here things I keep secret even from myself.
I hear in the creek not kept secrets but a keeping secret.
I am not dead, but nothing names more exactly what I am.

I hide behind my principles, and in my contradictions.
I don't know *what* I mean to tell you, I only know *how much*.

How much more this makeshift well cover reveals than it conceals:
consider that my subject here. Consider it a figure
for the unity of all, which I want to, but don't, believe.
For frame, four roughly equal lengths of two-by-eight, butt-jointed,
roughly square. Across it, rough boards that look to be barn siding,
salvaged, surely, from what once just sagged but since has fallen in,
what substituted for structure a scattering of shingles
around a neat array of rust-stunned implements, weed-worried.
Wide boards, moss-misted and splitting, splaying away from the frame.
No one here now knows who was here then, or even when *then* was,
when someone fessed as his present own our final fecklessness,
saw as distinctly then of what *would* happen that it *had to*
as we see it now of what *did*, understood the entailment
if barnslump then barnbuckle, knew when and with what to make do,
knew that what no longer met one need might yet meet another.

Another would approach these matters differently than I have.
There's appeal, for instance, in compiling lists of instructions.
Listen less to principles than for rhythms and symmetries.
Silence and conformity mortar the walls of the castle.
Loose syllable, word out of place: it matters, Mr. Crawford.
Never stand on the top three rungs of an extension ladder.
Don't infer from butterflies and birds that beauty is *attached*.
Meet a flank attack with a counterattack in the center.

Assuming sorrow has an outside does not make it so.
Ward away others' value-blindness by warding off your own.
To know his thoughts, to anticipate his actions, find his fears.
Connect positive to positive, but negative to ground.
Prepare to evacuate, should flash flood warnings be issued.
Refrigerate after opening. Die all, die merrily.
Speak? Love, and be silent. Behold the junipers shagged with ice.

Ice as it breaks up registers the creek's current, in the speed
at which free-floating fragments pass, but also in the angle
at which caught sheets project above the fallen log that snagged them,
its incidence determined by a boulder the last glacier
left here for the next, susceptible to the relentlessness
of *liquid* water in its shape, but not in its location.
I know this snagslant of these ice sheets is Message the Second,
but so what? I don't know from that what Message the Second is.
I'm sure, Dionysodorus smirked, that no speechless thing speaks.
But, Ctessipus countered, you can't be sure all things are speechless.
You can't be sure the ice (this ice, any ice) is not speaking,
in the suddenness of its self-assertion (this morning here
after last night not), in the variety of its voicings
(we call whalesong singing, though we can't translate what we hear sung,
why not icesong?), in the patterns of the bubbles it pretends.

Pretense does differ from purport, though less as one face differs
from another than as a death mask differs from the face that
(dark horse, dark rider emerging from thick fog) frowned it forward.

Hammered gold and gold enameling. Repoussé: from the French
pousser, to push. I've known not one emperor, never once been
to Athens to address Agamemnon mask to mask, but damn
I'm drowsy. Busy others buzz, augmenting reality,
the given having proven for them a little too little,
though for me it keeps proving much too much. As how could it not:
me, the overmatched, the not just not enough but not *nearly;*
it, the not just more than *me* by a mess but more than *itself.*
I am my own hired mourner. In place of mashing foil to face
I press my metaphysic of fog bank against a civics
of repousséing rider and horse. I differ from myself,
though not as portrait from sitter, not along just one axis.

Access denied. Keep moving. Two modes of one futility:
fact and command. To which I submit only under protest,
but to which I *do* submit, as they submitted, those stoop-shades
whose initials my name bears, whose posture and gait my body.
As their failures then forced them, so now mine force me to move on,
small town to smaller, bank loan to attic flat to rattletrap.
Some few appear, the rest of us disappear, into the world.
This is not the *story* of my life, but the *logic* of it.
Not a sequence of events, but an order of entailment.
Not Pilgrim's progress, but the view out Homebound's basement window.
Not Marvel hero overcoming close calls, vexing villains,
but archaic torso attending the stillness of stillness,
the secrecy, secret even from itself, that keep secrets
in secret. What must be listened *for* but can't be listened *to,*

what acts in what we *don't* do, proves itself in what we *can't* know.

No questions asked, no quarter given. No flash photography.
No vacancy. No tipping. No shoulder next seventeen miles.
No postage necessary if mailed in the United States.
No parking. No unregistered guests. No running in the halls.
No partially hydrogenated oils. No unauthorized
personnel. No pets. No measurable precipitation.
No dice. No part of this publication may be reproduced
in any form or by any means without prior written
permission from the publisher. No exceptions. No free rides.
No use. No one under the age of 21 admitted.
No problem. No strings attached. No more cookies for you, young man.
No unaccompanied minors. No shoes, no shirt, no service.
No heavy lifting for the next six weeks. No risk, no reward.
No guts, no glory. No excuses. No more Mr. Nice Guy.
No loitering. No smoking. No cholesterol per serving.

Persevering seems a less important principle during
my episodes of fading out, the moments (those standings-up
too suddenly) when everything recedes, myself most surely.
I *think* they're moments (they *feel* brief), though maybe, like Socrates'
or Silas Marner's, they're hours. I think them, too, *my* episodes,
but why not say that in my absence other lives multiply,
metamorphose this plentied world into one *more* populous,
better because more densely butterflied, less tenuously.
Hesperiids are the true skippers, sturdy, medium-sized,

short-winged. *Skippers,* for rapid, unpatterned, unprincipled flight.
Broad heads that bear at the base of the antennae tufts of hair.
The distal portion of the club is most often uncinate,
the flagellum clavate and narrowed. Some varieties have
scaleless patches on their wings. At rest they hold their wings closed, but
after death hesperiids fold their wings beneath their bodies.

Beneath our bodies, body. Within them, body. But *of* them?
If of those hesperiid bodies flight that fertilizes
profuse grasses and sedges, then of our human bodies what?
Landfill, oil spill, dustbowl, ground zero, all the aftereffects
that after the fact we euphemize as externality,
collateral damage, growth, truth and reconciliation.
But also small-scale meanwhile what-nots that vanish into those:
garage sales with pilled flannel baby pajamas piled beside
percolators and shoeboxes (sharpied *FREE!*) filled with eight-tracks,
and (their equivalent lamentation) *this,* this measured speech,
this pretense that one pattern, pursued persistently enough,
can if not outline yet index the presence of another.
Though not what the thunder said, this is what I would not have heard
had I not been listening for that. Not lightning-lit nightscape,
but the after-a-flash breathing out of the breath held during.

During loss should become, but never quite becomes, *after* loss.
My instep arch not only keeps the ache, it keeps the pressure.
Revealing what this loss is loss *of* hides what it is loss *to.*
My bones' ache sisters, whispers to, the ache of my soft tissue.

Tell me what you lost last, I'll tell you what you will lose next.

My aches make material my immateriality.

Mundane losses should prepare me for ultimate loss, but don't.

My aches migrate, joint to muscle, muscle to joint, while I sleep.

Revealing what it is I have lost conceals what loss itself is.

Like stone replacing downed wood, my aches are replacing my sleep.

Tell me how you lost the first, I'll tell you how you'll lose the rest.

My aches cross over me as voices carry across water.

Prior losses should, but don't, warn me away from future loss.

Loss opposes to what I experience what I perceive.

Tell me my loss is like yours. I tell you, it's like no other.

Other than the other than itself, little so abruptly,

with such indifference, deflects me. With such severity

as my studio window imposes upon sparrows am I

imposed upon by it. Let this not so much narrate impact

as attest to my sparrowlikeness. I did not so much hear

the thud as feel in my hollow bones its reverberation.

Which implies I neither felt what I felt nor heard what I heard.

Nor was what I was when I thought I was anything at all.

I cannot assert, but would never deny, identity

between the always already and the larger than itself,

or its contrary, difference between grounded and grounding.

It's now, when all is so still I could hear myself whisper,

that I dare not. It's because so soon all will be just as if

I'd never been, that all already is as if I were not.

It's now that I am most myself that I am not in the least.

Not least because perception is a kind of *work* do I count.
Not least because I feel accountable to coruscation
have I maintained this so long list of luminosities.
We don't get to *choose* whether what might elsewise glint gets obscured
by mist or dust, or which obscurity we resemble most.
My principles prove easier to profess than to fulfill.
Now it's *my* past, too, that moss-made-over makeshift well cover.
I've started over often, but never once stopped the counting
that began in my girlhood, of spiraling cones darker gray
than the surrounding gravel, of fast-fossiled meteorfish.
This is not the *story of* my life, but a *figure for* it,
not stars themselves, but the constellations I construct from them.
This is not the sum of coal cars, not their seriality,
not their noisy self-assertion, but what that second snowfall,
the one they bluster back into brilliance, tells me of the first.

Candescences

Less of my life happens by moonlight than happens as if by moonlight, reflected from something at once brighter and hidden. What I see by, I cannot see. What happens, or would happen, by wandering, happens as if by wandering. I myself would happen, if I could happen, as if by wandering. At this time of morning, when for hours yet morning still will stay night, still will stay still, in this hard season in this bleak town, these streets stay empty of people, especially of me, empty me in rubber boots and mismatched gloves. Empty of people, the streets, but not empty. Not empty of foxes, for example, who if they notice me never let on. **If they were more wary, I might feel more real, more myself.** More a self, any self. I thought with all this walking I would locate something, and *what* I would locate would be myself. Instead, each spent breath shimmers and dissipates, and I follow that countdown, those ephemeral intensifications reflecting again what has been reflected already off moon, cloudscrim, snow.

I mistrusted the thought that moves forward, sure of sequence, to the next thought, the thought that follows and *must* follow, but also casts back, keeps to itself the crusted thought that preceded it, without which it could not have been thought. Without which nothing could have been thought. **We had to climb into the trees before we could climb down from them.** What were our nails like, and our knuckles, when we climbed? Were these our knuckles now conferred on us by climbing? What did our voices evoke when we called across? To whom were we calling? Did other voices echo ours? Calling back to us, or warning one another? Which counts as our first thought, the climbing, the calling, or the being called back to? Of any sky it's true: no sooner askew with fruit bats than alert with eagles. No fruit bats here to flatter my late-night walks, but you should

33

see the sky, which is itself, and makes the snow, as the foxes' eyes must be to see so well at night, crystalline.

Names of godforsaken places: Burkburnett, Walters, Okemah, Cotton, Okfuskee. Names of children who overcame croup and quinsy but not all of whom the whooping cough allowed to pass: Roy William, Eva Anna, Della Mae, Clyde Edwin, Earl Glenn, Florence Evelyn, Betty Lee, Joy Aileen, Lois Wendel. In that order by birth, by death some other order I don't know, but doesn't so much matter, one and all done in now, whooping cough or no. Ways she made ends meet after first one husband died and then the other: managed a hotel, ran a furniture store, took in laundry. Help she got, and from whom, at each husband's death: two thousand bucks from the Kentucky Highway Department after a bridge he was helping build collapsed on the first, nothin from nobody after the second dud expired. Such short lists they sum to, those facts, once prolific, now scarce. **Such unsatisfying answers they evoke, these my graceless questions.** Did the facts of her life disappear behind this quilt, or survive in it? Am I, is it, recalling a life when I wrap my legs with it to read? Is it recalling her *life*, to recall these few facts from it? Does their being fewest make *her* least, or *me*? What I remember of her beyond what has been remembered to me: knee-high hose, a glass bowl glamorizing glossy stones, a rickety porch swing. Generations after mine that remember of her anything at all: none.

Is there a way to fix the defective gate? I keep oiling hinges, tightening loose screws on the latch, but winter here is long. Once rust settles in, it's insistent as mice in the shed and the cellar. The latch is loose because winter here wears the fence weak as rock: water seeps in, silvers to ice, soon the boards split, sure as boulders split, just faster. They don't need glaciers, these boards of low-grade, loose-grained pine. Maybe others can swing sturdier pickets, or just hire better contractors. My attempts at maintenance don't help: tightening the screws only speeds things along. Not that speed alters certainty. **Ice, necessity's best assistant, entropy's preferred deputy, never hurries, doesn't have to.** One day, you notice that what once was whole has split, and what wasn't loose, is. Not that there's no compensation: even here inside the house I hear the hinges when a visitor enters the yard, or would hear if anyone ever visited. I could hide then with cause, not, as I hide now, just in case.

My nightmares do wake *her,* even when they don't wake *me,* because I cry out. Sometimes *No! No!* but more often just inarticulate screams. I cry out, *and* I shudder and twitch and kick. **I try to keep my interiority interior, keep my dread to myself, but with little success when I'm awake, even less when I sleep.** Doesn't help that when my screams and kicking *do* wake me, the waking *out* of a dream happens always as a waking *into* it. Though not itself something I fear, armed men breaking into my home to murder me must figure something I fear. Maybe figures everything I fear. But so what? Happens a lot, this fitfulness, in those my age and gender. Though the rotting out by fear proves harder to measure and document. Even to detect, until too late. As, after all, when is it not? That rot is no armed man, exactly, and isn't breaking in, quite, but against it, too, I manage no resistance more effective than tremors and cries, disturbances of my sleep made disturbances of hers.

I always figured earlier in life I'd fall in love again later. I figured by then it couldn't much matter whether love lasted long or turned out well. One last love, not so different from one last house. So I don't pay off the mortgage, so what? **Now it *is* later, and I'm having second thoughts.** As who would not, who had to lock the door not to keep burglars out but to keep a six-foot six-year-old in. One who can count but not spell, run but not play. Can't save love for a rainy day, that I learned from my first love, though I guess I should have known going in. Doesn't portion well. Still, about that one last late-in-life house: give me a golf-course view, at least, if not a view of mountains or sea. Nothing fancy, just one unneighbored line of sight and a long hallway for my mathematical but anaesthetic second self to run and run (… 89 … 90 …). Vinyl siding and seamless gutters I can manage without, but I do want a big basement, in case I take up model trains.

Back to those foxes, though, that don't pay me no never mind. No separation of the last two words. Dactylic accent: NEVermind. It's what she would have said and how she would have said it, my ex-wife's brother-in-law's half-sister, with whom she was close before she passed. She my ex-wife, close with she the half-sister who passed. I think. They looked a lot alike, it's been years, my memory plays tricks. That voice, though, that accent, who could forget? Those figures of speech, that lilt. Regional dialects have gone for good, like the languages of gobbled-up small-scale societies, but God they were gorgeous while they lasted. The foxes on my late-night walks disappear, too, but only behind fences or between cars. Disappear from my sight, not from the earth. **So as to evoke but not fulfill desire for transcendence.** I'm not saying things as clearly as I'd like. Or as beautifully as I would say anything I said if I could recreate her accent. Her accent, and its sister gestures, arthritis be damned. I'm awkward in how I speak, and awkward, too, in how I walk. I blame it on the boots, but let's just say it's not much like the silkstride of those foxes. Not hardly, she'd say.

Doesn't take me long from here to reach the river. OK, not so much a river as a creek. **Drainage ditch, really, but I was taught not to fuss, taught to like what I**

got, pretend it was plenty, say thank you as if I meant it. I got little enough, six-packs of tube socks from my grandmother, or gloves or, worse, galoshes. She started in January, spent the whole year's Saturdays at garage sales, gathering gifts guaranteed to disappoint her greedy grandchildren, all of us instructed in leftovers and hand-me-downs, all reminded that when *they* were children, our parents had to rinse the jar, *drink* the last of the jelly. *Waste not,* and all that. The ditch, though, once it's frozen over, each first gust covers it in snow, each second blows it clear. All winter long a featherless biped heavy of foot, galoshes or not, would fall through the tenuous, contour-lined ice, but even early in the season, even late, those light-footed foxes glide right across.

What would I hear in my head if not those old hymns, what at night if not the trembling of trestles and rails under trains? Dull trestles, shiny rails. *Then sings my soul,* and so forth. I seldom get to listen *to* what I listen *for,* but for whom is that not true? And of what? **It's not hymns themselves for which I hanker now, it's what they hymn.** I don't remember all the words, or recall all the voices I heard repeating them, can't picture now all the Butler buildings and concrete-block rectangles I was taught to call sanctuaries. How think of it, how swiftly that world dimmed, except as practice for how swiftly this one's dimming? Or as evidence that this world has dimmed already. Evidence, of which there's plenty else: that twigs, too, fall in autumn, for instance. They don't turn golden first, and glancing out across the lawn you wouldn't notice them, but rake a pile of leaves and there they are.

Not that the suddenness with which it began gives grounds for hope it will ever end, but it *was* sudden, how it started. Rushing from the gate at which my first flight had arrived late, to the gate from which my next had departed already on time, from *no other way in* to *good luck getting out,* I started seeing unfamiliar faces (strangers passing me in the other direction) as familiar ones. Just like that, that man, never mind his loosened tie and unbuttoned collar, does not only *look like* but might *be* Dallas Hart, my dumbshit labmate in high school chemistry. That woman with the patterned shoulder bag doesn't just resemble but *is* Erin Martin, who waited tables to keep her kids in diapers while I bussed those same tables to put myself through school. Erin, dead now twenty years at least, and to whose kids God knows what happened after. **Changes how the airport feels.** Changes the grocery store here where I live, changes the streets.

I know it's true of any fox that I see it only when it lets me. But that poses me a question I don't *want* to know the answer to. If I see the fox when and because I mean nothing to it, does my seeing all I see prove I mean nothing, period? I perceive, therefore I am not, this steady scuffing of these scruffy rubber boots over these my neighbors' snow-slurred, root-buckled sidewalks notwithstanding. **These late-night walks give me time to work out my worries, but they also give me extra worries to work out.** Cats vanish beneath parked cars, the fox vanishes behind them. In either case, they give me to know (perhaps just are the knowledge) that I myself have vanished. I don't assume that their so erasing me erases others, but I do remark this separation they impose on my senses: I hear them often at night, cats and foxes alike, and I see them sometimes, but I've never yet heard one that I could also see.

Never used to happen, these nosebleeds. Out of nowhere now, though, often, and for no reason, or for no good reason. I don't have a long commute like my old schoolpal Christ. Short i. Not long i Christ as in the Messiah, son of Our Lady of Diphthongs and Drive-Through Package Stores, *that* Christ, to whom he bore little resemblance then and bears (despite his beard) even less now, but short i Christ, diminutive of Christopher, his given name, though no one ever called him that. Surely no one these days does, either. Not a Christopher type. His mother just guessed wrong. Must have wanted something else than what she got, as what mother does not, assign her begotten what name she will. Christ's commute, get this, it's two hours. Each way. Six days a week. Atlanta. Imagine. I'd get nosebleeds every day, all the violent history of imperial conquest condensed into symptom, expressed as thin cartoon mustache on my thin upper lip. **I'd keep tissues in the glovebox, then, besides the ones I keep in my jacket pocket now.** I'd buy them on sale, those shrink-wrapped three-box bundles. Not for tears. I don't cry often. I'd feel guilty: I'm beneficiary of all that violence, not victim. The nosebleeds, though, I can't control. Interpret or diagnose, they're bad news either way.

Having hymnals didn't help us harmonize, any more than sitting in rows did, on those hardwood pews. Since then I've learned it wasn't only us: not many souls can match a pitch. Words we managed fine (there they were to read and, besides, we had the hymns by rote), but not notes. *Just a closer walk with Thee.* **I have no answer now for what back then I didn't even know to ask.** If there's system to what we do insist must justify itself and what we don't, I can't see it. No one else seemed to notice how badly we all sung, and anyway there always was some precocious girl, the one exception, who because she *could* sing was called on often for solos, during which, for effect, she closed her eyes at high notes and drawn-out syllables. The hymnals were not gilt-edged (as our leatherbound, name-stamped Bibles were), but edged in rust-red, as if they'd been rudely spray-painted. The oldest women cooed the most over the girl's voice. Now she's in their place, her granddaughter is in hers, and they, the women who were oldest then, are in no place at all. As I myself soon will be, and in effect (these my declarations declare) already am.

No pattern to those recollected faces, or no pattern I can figure out. The face imposing itself over another face might be of someone close: my oldest friend, my long-time collaborator, even my beloved. Or of someone new, someone I barely know: the neighbor from a few blocks off who always pauses on her walk from work to reach over the fence and scratch my dog's ears. Or of someone I don't know at all: the overweight man I used to see at the park, not walking his chihuahua but sitting on a bench, holding the dog tight to his chin. Might be a face I only know from portraits: Paul Morphy, a bust of blind Homer, ecstatic St. Teresa. Might be a face of greed or grace: Margaret Thatcher, Wangari Maathai. No pattern I detect except that the ghosting happens *always*. **No face now does not propose some other.** No face but masks and is masked. I'd like to think this incessant substitution means I see into others' souls, or to the outer limits of my own, but it's more likely a correlative of tinnitus: another relentless beckoning by my partial decay toward my complete.

There's a limit to how high you can go, how high anyone has gone, with stone, but no limit to how much light you can let in. Maybe we *stumbled on* more than *invented* the arch, but someone had to see its implications, how it makes the gap as strong as the rest of the wall, makes the inside as bright as the outside, makes what we see by something to build with, something we can stain to make our stories radiant. See by, put by: *that's* the merger those cathedral builders brought about, the one I'm after here. Not to house God, but to see by what I put by and to put by what I see by. **I see the by and by, by the way, more often than I used to.** I don't sing about it now the way we used to then (the echoed "in the sweet"

40

never quite harmonizing with the first), but I see it much more vividly. It's implied by all I stumble on, and by my stumbling so frequently. And by my upper lip, nosebleed or no, staying chapped, less because it's dry here than because I'm forever biting my lower. Should have gotten braces as a kid, others did, but it was more than my parents could afford, and now I have bigger flaws to fix than crowded teeth.

Their legs are black, those foxes, and the backs of their ears, and their whiskers and eye sockets. Not that I'd know from those I spot on my walks, since I don't get close enough, not hardly, and of course they don't look at me, or anyway don't let me see them when they do look. In photos, though, it's as if they wear eye liner, lots of it. As sometimes I myself do. **Not thinking I can make myself fox-like, but as a kind of camouflage, a way to blend in, to *not* be seen as what I am, not see myself, not be seen *as* myself by anyone else.** Others here wear camo, too, most so they can wait in the cold for an elk. To take down one of which, I'm told, gives a thrill. I don't doubt that, but neither do I plan to try. It's true I wouldn't want to be the elk, front legs folding first, hind legs following awkwardly, but mostly I don't need to be cold any longer or more often than I am already.

That unasked-for transformation of unfamiliar faces into familiar: it's why I take my walks so late at night. And why in daylight I avoid eye contact with drivers when I'm on my bike. **It's not always people I've known who reappear.** It can be, say, a man I passed once on the sidewalk in San Francisco, twenty years ago, whose face I could not by intention and force of will have recalled, or the woman whose face I followed through four rooms of the Rijksmuseum on my first visit there. Sometimes the called-up face calls up such scenes, the circumstances in which I saw the face the single time I saw it, but sometimes not. Sometimes the face makes me see what surrounds it, or what surrounds me, differently as well, but sometimes not. Sometimes it just imposes the feeling I have seen it somewhere before. All the faces, though, assemble as the sense that I pass through a haunted rather than an inhabited world, a world I myself haunt rather than inhabit.

I once took for a claim on sound sleep what now I know was merely purchase. **What I've been calling late-night walks I should call early-morning, since I take them *after* sleep rather than before.** After what counts for sleep, which, these days, for me, means anything besides those nightmares, anything that ends elsewise than my crying out and kicking her awake. More late nights than not (more early mornings), after sleeping little and instead of sleeping well, I walk, but my alternative is a walk's equal and opposite: one morning in four, more or less, I sit in the shed. The foxes in the street already knew to pay me no mind, the mice in the shed soon learned. I myself learned what otherwise how would I know, that neglected things glow. Folding chairs, duffel bags, clay saucers and pots, loosely-looped fifty-foot orange outdoor extension cords, shovel, rake, handsaw, mud-stiff garden gloves, gas can, heater filters, trash bags, window screens, rusting cans of petrifying paint. It's not darkness those candescences defy, exactly. I *feel* rather than see them. As must the mice.

I don't need to be told what they entail ultimately, so I don't care to have explained to me what they signify meanwhile. "They" here designates the floaters in my eyes, which grow ever more frequent, active, imposing. They merge sometimes, starting as separate, paired and symmetrical, but expanding, stars exploding each into the other, brightness not dissipated by distribution across more space. They are their own opposites (loser and lost, atrocity and reconciliation): presences when I close my eyes, absences when I open them. The floaters don't wander but they do pulse, professing that I bear within myself the spectrum: when the central mass glows green, its fringes shift through yellow to red; when the sea asserts purple, its shores shift through blue to green. Turns out I *am* the night sky, in miniature, in secret, and (the cause of this my fretting) very much sped up.

Even inscrutable architecture bears measure, and is borne by it. No difference but this, that there, in the inscrutable, numbers keep to their own kind. Condylobasal length: 120-150 mm. Total length: 800-1100 mm. Weight: 5.0-9.0 kg. Means nothing to me, either. Means something to somebody, just doesn't mean to me whatever it means. *That* I'm used to: most things prove inscrutable to me. **Numbers keep to themselves; they seldom show me anything of what those hymns that haunt me now all hinted way back when.** *Then sings my soul,* we sang, none of us except that one tinsel-tonseled girl quite making the interval from *my* to *soul.* Back then responsibilities got imposed on me so often and so variously that it's no wonder I mistook indicative for imperative. I still hear *consider all the worlds* as a command, though one no longer issued by that pew-queued chorus, all those ill-fitted voices, each a pinch off pitch, no match for Bonnie Mifflin's. Bonnie, of whom now I recall only the fact, not the person.

But back to that bent-back light by which I am myself bent back into the part of me already, a long time back, bent back. Each night that light is new, and its renewal makes each night new, so each night walking through it I assign it a new name. Curtainaceous. Fox populi. Starslurry. Windmastered Walmart bag. **(It has a *sound*, the moonlight in this bar-stubbled town, the way a gustflustered plastic bag has a sound, even a voice.** Mostly keeps to itself, as does much else here, but speaks when it will.) Halotrailer. Gorse whisperer. Given over. It's not my naming the moonlight every night, though, that tells what there is to know about my noctigression, but that, tensing that naming back, Herakleitos-like, upon myself, I worry over its names for me. My not believing that moonmalleate light actually assigns me names doesn't keep me from caring what those names would be if it did.

Addendum to the list of what glows against that darkness in the shed: doorknobs. A dozen at least. In a drawer, nightstand-sized but by itself, the nightstand it once fit gone now who knows how long, who knows where. Glass doorknobs. Beveled. **No use now, but who could throw them out?** Not me, not after God knows how many homeowners past have abandoned them here. How could I not leave them to the next in line? We may last longer, each of us who haunts this house a while, than any generation of these mice, but we replace one another just as surely, and we're no more distinguishable from one another than they are. The ancients would have insisted on some source for the light that even in such pitch dark these doorknobs facet, that the eyes of these mice animate. I'm more concerned with destination. I wonder where it goes, this doorknob-diffracted light, and I worry where they have gone, those who have led wherever I am following.

Because crows stay the winter here, I see plenty I'd rather not see. All littlest things, don't let's exaggerate or dramatize, nothing ever on the order of what others see, what others suffer, every day. Squeamishness contributes to, cannot be isolated from, my larger moral failures. Still, "picked clean" does not well describe a post-crow carcass, nor even "picked apart," quite. "Picked *down*" would be more apt, or "picked flat." **It's still one thing, just leathern, eyeless, eviscerated.** I used to try not to avert my face, as if a face turned toward any one thing were

Steph:

I hope things are better at Harvard than they are out here in the hinterlands. UW continues to try to lead the way in straitening higher education with neoliberal policies and reactionary ideals.

I hope, too, that you will find things to enjoy and value in the enclosed. You'll know that they appeared in print almost simultaneously not because they were written together but because independent press publishing does not exist solely to cater to my whims.

This brings greetings of peace and health.

not averted from all else. This happens to me often, no hope of stopping it, that some quality I embrace as courage I recognize later as metaphysical misunderstanding, a way to use the world to fool myself about myself. In this case with help from the snow, which hides those carcasses from me, saves them for small but numerous scavengers (insects, microbes) to finish, come spring.

Snow covers the carcasses, but cannot hush them. Not hardly. **Not when they speak to me, as they do, as I protest *everything* does.** The old car radio used to could catch KMOX (that's how *she* would say it, my ex-wife's brother-in-law's half-sister, "used to" like "Houston" apocoped down to no h or n), if it was late enough at night and far enough away from wherever I'd been or thought I was headed. Happened often enough back then: late shift, the kind of tired that meant no point heading straight home, couldn't expect to sleep. That car radio's long gone to its rest, gotta do for myself what catching I can, which turns out to be plenty. Signals from those crow-gutted carcasses, from grocery carts rattling over blacktop, from sliding doors on delivery vans a block away, from one live oak wide enough to need propping at each elbow. Signals from all that signals me, and nowadays nothing does not.

If those signals reached me even *there* and even *then*, surely some inept is catching KMOX right now in Reykjavik or Montevideo, or, more like, in Laugarvatn or Orgoroso. For myself, for the moment, I'm after the crossing back that would reverse origin and destination. Good to listen *to* and listen *for*; how much better, then, to listen *across*? Why leave only the sent to carry? **They're my signals, too, now, so let the listening carry me to them as it has carried them to me.** In this I follow those adepts that on my late-night walks outsmart me, having taught themselves to haunt the both-and-neither (urban/rural, civic/wild, inhabited/abandoned) through which I wander, performing my disorientation. I don't know what they know, only that they know it. I do know they know things I don't. I would walk the signals back, after the spider walking her web. After the fox, both-and-neither predator/scavenger, as likely to carry back to her mewing kits a mouse or rabbit as a half-eaten ham-and-cheese.

In other words scavenging preys upon predation. In other words we have a maintenance issue on the aircraft and cannot begin the boarding process until it has been resolved. In other words we regret the condition in which your parcel arrived and we assure you that great care was taken in the handling of it. In other words all our customers are very important to us, so there will be a survey at the end of this call. In other words this call is being monitored. **In other words a rescue attempt would risk more lives than it could save.** In other words we have a name for this syndrome but no cure. In other words our exit strategy was flawed. In other words cause of death has not yet been determined. In other words this suicide note is just longer and more detailed than most. In other words you're bluffing and I've known it all along. In other words draining the marsh only made the flooding worse. In other words where the weather's *that* bad sending up a signal flare won't help, not hardly. In other words I'm not having the test done because I know it would tell me something I don't want to hear.

Or that one Sunday morning service when a man walked naked into the sanctuary. That's what we called it, the sanctuary, though those rows of pews, that plain-curtained baptistry backing up the pulpit, didn't so much signal sacredness as create consensus in support of seeking excess of meaning in a dearth of cues: looking for the Invisible, listening for the Inaudible. Whole thing happened during a prayer, so hardly anyone knew. That the sanctuary had industrial carpet in the aisles, that the man had bare feet, meant all that sudden movement happened quietly. He wasn't noisy, just naked. It was the offertory prayer: a row of deacons in dated suits and fat-knotted rayon ties stood at the front facing the congregation. (That's what we called collecting money, the offertory, and what we called ourselves, the congregation.) **We'd been bidden to bow our heads, but I didn't always.** (The way *she*'d say them, those two rhyme: we'd been bidden, but I didden.) Just took a couple of deacons to hustle the intruder out, quietly, before the prayer was over. Gave me time to close my eyes and bow my head, so no one who hadn't seen the naked man saw that I had.

Not the victim's real name. Not nothing, but not much, certainly not enough. Not "tenderness toward existence," because not turned *toward*. **Not how things are supposed to happen, not how things were supposed to end.** Not at all. Not so damaging, not so vicious, as divorces go, but still did not feel good. Not guilty. Not negotiable. Not a possibility this time, not for you a possibility ever. Not my type. Not the right address. Not the winning ticket, not even close. Not bad for a first effort, but don't expect to be invited back. Stunt double, body double, double down. Not what the forecast called for. Not what I ordered, not what I expected, not what I was promised. Not sturdy enough a coop to keep out raccoons, but blood and feathers assert a certain beauty, scattered over snow. Not that I would try to stop you, but you're *sure* that's what you want to do? Underneath the seat in front of you, or in the overhead bin. Not now. Not a nightingale, but plenty beautiful for me. Not until you're *not* happy will you discover that you *were*. Not until too late will you meet your one true love. Not prudent, but I don't regret it. Not one bit.

I didn't think at the time to wonder what a balm was, or where Gilead, just let it sound good. I didn't think to wonder who might have put two syllables into the "there," or whether that spare syllable might archive experience far beyond my slim experience, pain beyond what little pain I'd known then. It was a song suited to mismatched baritones, awkward in collared no-iron shirts, not one to feature Bonnie Mifflin's larklikeness. I wonder plenty now, though, not because my pain parallels those ur-singers' pain, but because I do know now of pain at least one thing I didn't know then, that it returns. Not *from* somewhere, not because it ever goes away, just returns. **Goes away no more than, but returns as surely as, the moon-drawn.** Maybe *is* moon-drawn, why wouldn't it be. Their devastating pain must have returned then, my stubborn minor pain does now. Returns sometimes to my joints and muscles, often to my neck and head and lower back, always to my teeth. As a fallen tree trunk turns with perfect patience into stone, so I, balmless biped, am becoming my pain. Am become.

Not everything I say here is true. Not much is. Though if that surprises you, stop now, pour yourself a shot of hundred proof, settle in to some sitcom reruns. If you've trusted me until now, do not pass go. But here's a proposition to put money on. When it gets this cold, my car won't start. It's old, and I've got no garage, so it sits out overnight. Good thing I can walk to work. Not that *that's* a perfect solution. Sidewalks stay ice-glazed here, I'm old enough to teeter, and bearing a book-burdened backpack makes me top-heavy. Sometimes I trip and flail forward, sometimes I slip and fall on my ass. Apparently I *shuffle*. I learned the hard way, but I learned: I have to remember to lift my feet when I pass old trees whose roots have raised one sidewalk slab above another. Still, once the wind has carried its fury elsewhere, the snow, and even the cold itself, imposes a hush in which I hear voices otherwise shouted down, songs otherwhen overwhelmed.

I should have figured on the foxes' evanescing, should have preseen night wanderings as my trespassings on their range, not as theirs on mine. That's how you-know-who would have said it, *figured on.* Though she'd have said *shoulda.* Sheeda said. I shoulda figured our liminalities would parallel, shoulda known that foxes follow the fringes of ecotones: they thrive where scrub seams scree, say, or where forest finials field. And haunt the crepuscular, hunt more at dusk and dawn, when mice and rabbits most readily surrender. **Foxes move when their prey moves, as what predator does not.** Which, here in town, where fringes include alleys (all those clustered dumpsters and gathered-in garbage bins), translates not to twilight but to when most people are asleep. They're at work, then, the foxes, while I walk. As hush-hungry in their way as I am in mine. Less clumsy, though, and much better equipped: bigger ears, keener sense of smell, pads on their paws.

Didn't help, though, because in the dream she was on the bus already. I was supposed to be. **The plane wasn't going to wait for the bus, so the bus wasn't going to wait for me.** While it idled next to one building, I fussed in another, in a kind of commons room: laundry, kitchen, tv, big trash bins. The parking lot between was vast, like at a stadium or a mall. I don't know *how* I knew she was on the bus, but I *did* know, no less surely than I knew I was not. I was trying to pack, but I couldn't find everything. My suitcase was open, but my clothes were still out, wet. I'd washed them but not moved them to the dryer, so someone had piled them next to my open suitcase. I couldn't find my jeans, couldn't find my backpack, couldn't find my shoes. I heard the bus cough into gear and shudder to its start, but no way could I get to it. In the dream I was waving and yelling "Wait! Wait!" so of course I woke her with, and she woke me from, my kicking and crying out. What happens inside doesn't always stay in, any more than what happens outside stays out. Never did, but these days my God.

Wider than my outstretched arms. That maybe doesn't sound like much, since even a vulture's wings can spread five feet, and who doesn't see *them* all the time. But that's at a distance, soaring, so no difference, bigger than crows or not. This was a golden eagle, though, feeding. Wish I'd seen the stoop. **Never been so close before.** Fucker was *big*. Don't worry, I know the rules here, what will count and what won't in a report like this, what is permitted me to say and how it is permitted me to say it. My heart *does* ache, and a drowsy numbness *does* pain my sense, but never mind: you won't have to suffer my apostrophizing this bird, or any next. I was just in the car on a highway, not hiking backcountry. Still, we interrupt our regular programming. Long stretch of lonely road, 487 is through the Shirley Basin. Ravens waited their turn to tickle the kill. The eagle let me pass at 85 without regard, but watched warily when I came back, and lifted when I stopped. Clumsy at first, slow wingbeats, feathered legs dangling a second or two before they tucked. That bird, though, that big, that close to that road, you'd have turned around, too.

Not quite the way I would have, but someone before me in this house did a little fixing up and adding on. Not much up to code, must have done things themselves. **Who am I to criticize, though, I who have to hire out any home repair more complicated than an outlet cover.** When they made that useless dormer of the attic (thinking God knows what, since it's too narrow to accommodate a bed, too low to stand up straight in, got no closet) they stuck in a set of rickety stairs at one end (steep stairs, narrow treads, wildly uneven), but left the pull-down ladder in the hall. Long string dangles to a ping-pong-ball-sized brown rubber grip. You can pull the ladder down, but not climb up, because they built right over it. Covered the opening with subfloor: brand-stamped plywood, wrong-sized nails hammered through, taloned at rusty angles and irregular intervals. Like I say, though, not for me to judge: ten years I've haunted here, tilting my head to dodge the dangling ladder-pull every time I traipse the hall, and still I haven't cut the string.

Bad news either way, these frequent nosebleeds, no point going to the doctor. Takes no more-co-paid-than-covered, wait-a-few-days lab test to discover to me that I leak. I need someone who got good grades in private school to tell me my body's failing me? Someone too busy memorizing the periodic table to notice about time and tense that *is failing* and *will fail* have a half-grown love child named *has failed, always already*? Besides their grating-as-the-satan's-ambassador-buzzer-on-my-dryer reminder of my mortality, besides the signal they send that I carry as my very body an economy that demands I receive the constant upping of my deductible with gratitude for having health insurance at all, the nosebleeds are *inconvenient*. I can't grow a mustache, for instance. Not that I would want to, that's not the point. The point is *nothing* would be a good look for me anymore. The point is I can't move on *from* even these my trivial concerns, having nowhere to move on *to*. **The point is not this one incapacity, but that the list of its like, already long, keeps growing longer.**

All thumbs, she said of me, laughing, back when we laughed, then *thumb up your ass* later on. I've known people with one ear that sticks out more than the other, had a crush in school on a girl with one green eye and one blue, heard tell of extra nipples and too many toes, but one of my ears is *bigger* than the other. *Bigger by a barefoot crick crossin.* People notice. Try not to, but can't help themselves. *That one ear's biggern Maude's back porch.* I go to the same barber over and over, because that ear makes new ones nervous. As for her: she overlooked it for the longest, but not forever. There's a poetry to the fact of my fixed expression, *nerve damage*

51

they used to tell me when I used to ask, though damage in what sense I never knew, since those nerves were ever as they are now. There's a poetry to makeshift fences, to the tear gas we haves have our officers offer those irritating have-nots to keep them out. Make an orderly line, single file. Wait your turn. **Have your papers ready.** There's a poetry to this clip of refugees receiving instruction in the language of border patrol, a poetry to the reminder, in the gesture of blessing, of the gesture for halt.

Let him stand for all his like: the un-, the ill-, the simply seldom-remembered. By *him*, I refer to Hooper Skelton, who in a dickie of deacons stands still at the front of that one church into which all the many churches of my slurred childhood blur. (To disambiguate: I mean he continues to stand, not that he stands without movement, though that's true, too. Continues to stand, never mind the several decades since, in some one of which he must have died.) White shirt, thin fabric, size M instead of fitted to collar circumference and sleeve length, surely from the five and ten. Slicked-back hair. Kept the books for his younger brother's shoe shop on the square. (Another steadstander, that shop, for something different but still decades dead.) **One hand holds the other wrist as he listens through the offertory prayer.** His wife stayed home, the word for her then was *sickly*, though sickly in what way who knew. Hooper Skelton himself never missed a Sunday, never rotated off the roll of deacons, never replaced that one brown suit (so serious about itself, slacks pleated and cuffed), that one clip-on bow tie, or even, what you'd think, that one brown pair of plain-toe oxfords.

Another thing I should get fixed: the gutters on the shed. (Tense again. Shoulda gotten fixed.) **Not for a single major failure, but for several small.** One downspout teeters, gutter to splash block, nowhere secured to the clapboard. At the other corner on the same side of the shed, no downspout at all. Of course that corner should be higher, but it's not, so for hours after a rain and for days during snowmelt, there's a steady drip from the imperfect seam. Never mind that leaves collect, from which, because I don't clean often enough, seedlings sprout. Like I need another figure for my inconsequence. Whoever hung these gutters was no watchmaker's twin, everything just so. The main problem, though, the one I'm after here, is they're loose, so when I sit in the shed at night they rattle. A decent wind makes the rattling loud, and the wind here blows hard. Blows all the time, seems like. The mice hardly notice, but how could I not? So much noise does not *diminish* but does *compromise* the darkness, and (sit how long I will) makes the auras of gas can and garden hose a little harder to detect.

Or take the case of Oran Dinwiddie, red-haired, freckled, done in who knows how. I say one way, my older sister says another. I heard he worked on line repair and was electrocuted, she heard he fell from a moving car. Neither of us has any facts except second-hand, and we know we both of us remember badly, because she thinks she heard what she heard *from me,* and I think I heard what I heard *from her.* Neither event takes much to imagine. Never with Oran, but I did sit shotgun once or twice while some kid my equal in stupidity drove his Dad's car a little too fast, and one my superior in drunkenness leaned out the back window with his arm outstretched to flaunt a bottle he held by its neck. Same thing with the other possibility: from my one summer loading I-beams onto idling rigs I can extrapolate to fixing downed power lines for a living. **In this erasure, who is most erased?** Doesn't strengthen my sense of my own substantiality that I don't know how Oran Dinwiddie died, and that apparently there's someone else just as badly blurred, someone I and my sister both knew sometime back, but that any longer neither of us can even name.

Maybe my seeing faces from my past in the faces right in front of me means I should stop sneering at couples out to dinner, texting others instead of talking to one another. **Maybe it means some underneath of me, some south wind that someone less tetchy toward the term than I am, might call my *soul*, prefers absent to present.** Maybe it means only absence *ever* presents itself to me, means (what might follow) I am myself absent, even to myself. It does mean I saw yesterday, not twenty paces off, the face of Strecker Faudi, who in school never spoke when called on in class, who always wore a ski cap rolled up above his ears, who went to the principal rather than take off that cap when ordered to in German class by the teacher who deserved the nickname we thought ourselves smart for assigning her, Frau Schadenfreude. Strecker, who one day just lit out. I've never known if he worked, say, fishing boats or offshore oil rigs, don't know now if he lives neighborless in Idaho. Lives neighborless *somewhere*, though, I bet, and wouldn't want me nor nobody else to try to find out where.

Not that I haven't wondered whether the foxes that on my night walks show no fear of me are the same one fox or several different. **I'm not *so* incurious that I haven't tried to learn.** But how would I? From whom? Fox territories vary widely in scale, sized by food available in the given environment. But does this trash-lush small town's density of dumpsters, do its badly bin-blistered alleys, mean a fox needs not many blocks, and thus that each night I cross numerous territories, or do they mean the whole town offers barely sustenance enough, and my walk stays within one fox's turf? How would I find out? Google Maps doesn't display fox territories, and my librarian slips out to lunch if she sees me coming, time of day be damned. No use pressing her for help to suss another source I know in advance doesn't exist. (The social lives of even solitary animals prove complex.) I'll stick to impossibilities I can suffer by myself.

Tap tone'll tip you off, tell you long past and later on of a quartersawn sheaf of fine-grained spruce, whether the rootball strangled buried bells, what right embrace might yet release from it their ringing. Her glass ear'll guest list what all else. First distorts, then redistributes even this dingy light to let me read on these leak-rorschached walls whether she's nodding me yes or no, turning toward me or turning away. Seems like the umpteenth time I've changed my shirt, or oughta've. **Seems like I keep myself most often scarce.** I'd be *rumored,* but first somebody'd need to notice, then somebody else'd need to care. When I *do* show, I present as a streetlight-spotlit stranger, hat in hand, no hoo-ha but no news, either, from God or any of God's fellow far-offs. Bedrock here whispers radon, I'd listen with one of those tests if my house were tighter, if I weren't worried over certain words, like *vitreous,* like *iridectomy.* Lovebugs taunting the boxwood, shoo fly shoo. Blackbirds in the marsh call out all the time, but I *notice* only when one note goes missing. Some things that, and some times when, they say only owls can see, I say I see, too.

I know no proper name for either, so I've assigned each a name of my own. *Sobluenary*: after a stretch of cloud-muffled, snow-close days, a first night not, still dark plenty but now dark bright, overseen by a moon not full quite but full what the hell. *Rusty's*: wrecks, stacked three high, arranged in rows, defying the flood plain *and* the zoning laws that say don't tempt the hundred-year, don't ask for more trouble than we got already. In any former, I make a point to pass the latter, for their reminder (the two together) that any second-order disorder overorders its first. It's hard while I'm walking to count those squares of soblue snow sobering so many roofs of so many so junked cars, but harder not to, so I arrive each night at a different number, surely my error (the road out there is rough, no sidewalk, no shoulder, I have to watch my feet and stay ready to give way to headlights, not because anyone's out at that hour but just in case). Still, nothing prevents my excusing inconsistency by pretending those platonic squalids move: change places, come and go.

That's not what bothers me about the floaters, their pulsing, when they do pulse, at some rhythm other than my heart rate. Slower, so it feels tidal, even glacial, the centuries-indifference of ice sheets expanding and contracting. If they *only* pulsed, and *always* pulsed, I could account those floaters correspondences, corpse to cosmos, pretend them indices of my oneness with the One. Eventual oneness, oneness due soon if not done quite yet. Oneness hard-won. But sometimes, instead of pulsing, they *spin*. **I find no consolation in the consolations I'm offered.** I should feel better that so little time is left me, because nothing else lasts long, either? The floaters' spinning just extends the list of symptoms I withhold from the nurse taking notes. As does the appearance, sometimes, of satellites. Should I lament that I am not yet, or should I dread how soon I must be, outside the Outside? Spinning, the floaters seem smaller, more symmetrical and smooth, than when they pulse. Shinier, even, but their range of colors stays the same.

Instead. Unsteady. Bedstead. Homestead. Steadfast. Steady as she goes. I put my steed to stud not long before he went to seed, I've put him out to pasture since. **I'd propose an amendment, but the question has been called.** I fell in love with my limnologist less for her understanding of my lakes and wetlands than for her lisp. That, and her listing a little to my left. (Broken leg when she was a boy. Small-town doctor, needed a nip or two to steady his hands, set that bone as best he could, but it healed up crooked, tilted her a smidge off kilter. Not far, but enough that now anyone would know it's her, toting her tablet down the hall, TUMtaTUMta, left step heavy, right step light.) Augustine set down his confessions true north, but I've skewed these a little westerly because there's so much I'd as soon God didn't know. Or anyway didn't hear from me. None of her pet names for me so far starts with s. I'm hoping for Sisyphus, say, or Spinoza, though I'd settle for something simple as Sweets. So far, God's been lenient with my lies, hasn't pressed for relevance or consistency. She listens with her one good ear and lets them pass.

Allowing language for the medium of my inner life doesn't mean I can't declare myself the medium of its. **I don't, but not from modesty, and not because I doubt myself and language interleaved.** Leaves fall, lives fall (one unmiserly medium alleged), and sure enough every little while some new loss steads me in, or (more like) morphs me into, an emptier place. The decades since have blurred together all those sermons whiskered up from double windsors, but the hymns, all ponytails and pincurls, I remember one by one. *Very deeply stained within, sinking to rise no more.* Reverend Curtin's voice I can't recall, but Bonnie Mifflin's I still hear. *When nuh-uhthing else could help, love lifted me!* The curtains that preserved the baptistry private were olive green one year, harvest gold the next. Like refrigerators in the first flush of crushed-ice dispensers, like formicaed kitchen countertops (one ill-glued corner warping up loose), like shag carpet and melmac. They're all just words now: Bonnie, the baptistries, those plastic plates slick with canned asparagus. Which must mean, how could it not, that I'm become all and only words myself.

My insistently seeing faces that aren't there in place of faces that are has inaugurated this recurring nightmare: I'm trapped on the roof of a two-story house in a flood. A few other gables, each ringed with treetops and deckled with doves, are visible in the distance. Among the debris that registers the umber-colored current, bloated bodies float. Tree limbs and car tires and what-not drift by at random, but the corpses pass at regular intervals, in procession. And are identical. Or, more exactly, the bodies are indistinguishable, the same body again and again, bearing each time a different face. The sequence *(whose* faces, in what order) spells something out, as letters spell out words and words serry sentences, but whatever the dream faces (always blank, eyes closed) tell, they tell in some language I can't read. **They pass some judgment on my life, but not one I can understand or influence.** From *this* dream I don't awaken crying out or kicking, just cold, convicted not of *doing* wrong, but of *being* wrong.

She would say "She would say it as" as "How she would say it is." *She* here same as ever, my ex-wife's brother-in-law's half-sister, the one who sang without knowing it or meaning to, or (how someone smarter than me would say it is) the one whose speech was song already, without her trying to sing. How she would say it is "might should." She'd say "Might should check the cornbread" or "Might should buster back the crape myrtle a mite more this year." So. Me? Might should set aside something from each paycheck. Might shoulda been settin more aside all along. Might should slow down for school zones, come to a complete stop at stop signs, cops are quick with tickets here. **Might should take my car in, find out why that one warning light stays on all the time.** Might should clean the bathroom, might should mop the kitchen floor. Might should go easy with the butter on my toast, the salt on my eggs. Might should cut out caffeine and alcohol altogether. Might shoulda cut down a good while ago. Might should see about these stigmata, doctor might not tell me what I tell myself, though, that they're the marks on me of what marks all, the X of the ineffable.

Would have been plenty, the stoop my Dad handed from his Dad down to me, but I've got other small debilities and deformations for supplement. **One eye wanders when I get a little tired, which I do sooner these days than I used to.** One eyelid droops, all the time. And the knobby knuckles have begun, like little blisters on the backs of my finger joints. No more *citius, altius, fortius* for me. Not hardly. Not a complaint, though. I've looked around, I know *got things easy* when I see it. In fact, this is the point in the service when the organ would diapason the Doxology, for Bonnie Mifflin to lilt and the rest of us to bray. *Praise God from whom all blessings flow.* That I can't get rings on and off my fingers nowadays doesn't count as difficulty finding anchorage. Doesn't keep me from counting foxes on my walks, and the mice in the shed hardly notice, don't seem much to mind. Doesn't stop their scurrying over and around me. That one eye no longer opens all the way doesn't mean I can't detect the shimmer (think northern lights, just infinitely faint) from knuckle-worn, compost-crusted garden gloves.

Not that I expect to figure out just what conditions would have to hold across the cosmos for my mooncast shadow to win its nightly contest with those the street lights cast. We're a species, like foxes or mice, we who over time come to know less, not more. I don't wish I'd been that man walking naked into the cement-block sanctuary during Sunday services, or Hooper Skelton helping shoo him out. Aspiring to no other role, though, doesn't make me unashamed to have been the boy who had no hand in shaping what he saw. I've lost the virtues and courtesies those deacons inculcated, however surely the shame they shared stays with me. **Sometimes the floaters rise slowly one after another and dissipate, oil bubbles from a battleship downed decades back.** Might should note that to the nurse instead of keeping it to myself. Might should get a colonoscopy. Might should exercise three times a week (though it's a little late to start that now).

Might should sometimes fess up first, instead of always getting caught. Might should use live bait instead of lures. Might should pull the screens out of the shed. Stays so cold here so much of the year, I'd hate to miss a day when I can open windows.

Grit

[First...]   For *intemperate*, the reader may substitute *indelicate, inflexible, inveterate, inviolate, insatiate,* or any other four-syllable iambic word beginning with the negative prefix in-. Recall here (recall, indeed, throughout this entire work) the use of epithets in the *Iliad* and *Odyssey*, their application guided by rhythmic context rather than by denotative content. I defer here no more than Homer deferred there to *reference* as the exclusive source or arbiter of meaning. [...tell.]

[Tell...]   Try as one might to keep cosmology and morality apart, still they whisper sweet nothings to one another through a chink in the wall, forced separation transforming those sweet nothings into everything. *Strict,* from *strictus,* past participle of *stringere,* to draw tight, as in the strings string theory supposes as givers of gravitons, those faux-presocratic drawers-tight of all. [...fall.]

[This fall,...]   The math *itself* is mesmerizing, too, not only the results it generates.

$$f(x,y) = \begin{bmatrix} a & b \\ c & d \end{bmatrix} \begin{bmatrix} x \\ y \end{bmatrix} + \begin{bmatrix} e \\ f \end{bmatrix}$$

I need not have seen a fractal fern frond to find the frond-forming function fine.   [...hush.]

[*Hush,...*]   I have measured out my life with paper cups. Small white up-side-down-dunce-cap-shaped cups for clutching sno-cones in summer Bible

61

school; thimble cups at the dentist, for rinsing out grit after yet another numb-
ing, drilling, filling; cups in tidy rows atop blistered pressed-board folding tables along the route of the protest march, then a few steps later spilling over
trash-can liners; cups dispensed from a plastic tube attached to the bubble-vol-
uble water cooler in the otherwise mute waiting room...   [...long.]

[I long...]   Partner how often they will, parallel and perpendicular can't
avoid questioning by curvature, qualification by entanglement, compromise by
clinamen, as performed in this instance by "brocade," from the Italian *brocco*,
twisted thread. [...off.]

[Often...]   Only position *respect* high enough in the hierarchy of virtues,
and you can rationalize many of our boys' behaviors, maybe most, their worst
right along with their best: who they help, and when; who they bully and why;
why they like their pickup trucks so large and loud; why they insist on all those
guns (and insist on *showing off* their guns, not only on *having* them and *using*
them). But bear in mind that it's the respect, not the rationality, they pursue.
[...count.]

[I count...]   Structure, here as ever an effect of counting; shape, of calculation; meaning, of number simpliciter. Three porticos, one for each theological
virtue; eighteen spires, one for each apostle, one for each evangelist, one for
Mary, one for Jesus; pinnacle one meter less than that of Montjuïc. *Ascent*
serves for a spiritual metaphor frequently enough that no one has to *call* it sa-
cred, a steep climb up one of those spires, or *say* it twins kneeling in a stained-
light chapel.   [...trout.]

[Tryouts…]   My inability to reduce their relationship to something simpler (and smaller in scale) than this work in its entirety does not make them unrelated questions: Yi Lu's, whether the butterfly, alight on a leaf, is waiting or has given up; and mine, how to infer from what the fossil recalls to what it foretells.   […letter c.]

[I see…]   Actually it's the snail-shell-shaped cochlea, not the incus, malleus, or stapes, that fleshes the Fibonacci sequence and figures the golden ratio. Either way, structure *sings* because we *hear with* what we *see* as number. […second.]

[Second…]   Briefly resting butterfly and fully-rested fossil fish, longer side and shorter in a golden rectangle, A-side and B-side on a vintage 45, yes, of course. But here another relationship: the reciprocity between promise and secret. No secret more secretive than a promise, no promise more promising than a secret promise. Is that principle itself a secret or a promise? And this my obsessing over the principle, which is *it*?   […all.]

[All…]   As numbers ever want renewing, so too do words. If incursion into number can perplex a paradigm, surely borings into word can perforate one.   […night.]

[Night…]   My Latin never was any good, as my Latin professor would confirm, were she not now conversing facie ad faciem with Cicero. (To this day I can't call him Kickero without embarrassment.) Still, were this my "Ego Dominus Tuus," I'd have set to bickering not *Hic* and *Ille* but *Skeleton* and *Stoop,* and I'd have left it open which is master of which. But I'm no more Yeats than I am

Leibniz. (*I knew Bill Yeats. Bill Yeats was a friend of mine. Poet, you're no Bill Yeats.*) [...measure.]

[Measure up...]   No mechanical ringer in a brick-big analog trimline phone on my nightstand only means my premonitions must assume other forms. Only confirms me less like Marge in *Fargo,* susceptible to sudden summons from flanneled sleep to cold-batteried Prowler, than like Norm, forever measuring out that recalcitrant mallard that will never measure up to the Hautmans' tantalizing blue-winged teal.   [...message.]

[Message...]   Sometimes titles total: get the title right, no need to right the rest. As if to recuperate lost time. Toward recuperation of lost time. In memory of bygone times. Of times lost to memory. Because there's no reintegrating the disintegrated. To the restoration of time lost. To the recollection of the lost-to-time. Diggings-down toward buried moments. Present substitutes for long-lost pasts. Reappearances from times that disappeared. Replacements for the irretrievably perditioned. Perpetual present, past perditional.   [...mark.]

[Mark...]   A Dialogue of Self and Soul

I maintain and operate all the machines in the lab,
but don't know how to interpret the readouts they generate.

I hover over what I would immerse myself in.
I could map the terrain but can't mud-burden my boots in it.

I wouldn't sleep so fitfully if I didn't drink so much,

or drink so much if the pain in my joints weren't so sharp, so constant.

I am neither your sleep nor your sleeplessness, but I do measure the distance between them and commemorate your crossings.

Lying still, corpse pose, mitigates the dizziness and nausea.
I can't sing you to sleep, only sing to you in place of sleep.   [...the whole.]

[My whole...]   I claim as a generative ambiguity, that the Latin *vestigium* names both the sole of the foot and the *impression* of that sole, the footprint. Printer and printed. It makes the present enumeration of vestigialities (as it would make *any*) an investigation, from *vestigare,* the verb meaning to track, to follow footprints.   [...what-not.]

[Not that...]   The stability or instability of value, because it preoccupies me in life, will recur as a question throughout this work. All those years I lived in that woodstove-heated house, I groused about the same forever splitting and toting of logs, not to mention the always waking up cold, that now I recall wistfully. Does that make the value stable or unstable? And what does it say about me? Did I value it then without knowing I valued it, or did I only come to value it after the fact? Am I assigning different value to it now, or perceiving different values in it?   [...the latter.]

[The ladder...]   I take this opportunity to confirm what surely the reader suspects, that here (and throughout) the subject includes, the stakes involve, the unsaid sister to the said, not only the said itself. In this case, not just the one kid pond-drowned, but also the many merely pond-deprived. Whole childhoods, after which whole lives, without wading in rolled-up jeans, ankle-deep in murk, bare toes sieving soft fish-shit-slurried silt, childhoods zebco-zed-ded, never learning to leave half the worm free, to start at the head when taking hold of the palm-sized bluegill, smoothing back the dorsal fin to keep from being barbed. And in *con*firming the suspicion, to *af*firm any and all substitution by the reader of unsaid for said.   [...paint?]

[Pained...]   It helps to picture not the platform-stepped clattery aluminum extension ladder most typical today, but an old-fashioned dowel-runged creaky wooden straight ladder, not because it matters so much to the weight of the Wittgenstein cited here, or to make analogy with the different feel of a wooden roller-coaster from a metal one, but in preparation for the allusion, later, to Frost's speaker's feet keeping even into fitful sleep, the ache and pressure of the (wooden) ladder-round.   [...suddenly.]

[Suddenly,...]   Augustine takes my time-boundedness as the first proof of my finitude: I'm not God, because, unlike God, *my* past has departed, *my* present is without extension, and *my* future can never arrive. I worry that, too, but even more urgently I worry number-boundedness: I'm not God, because when the carnival comes to town, the weekend of the county fair, I have to *guess* how many brightly-dyed jellybeans dizzy the jar.   [...will.]

[Will...]   Same thing that happens when I sit happens even sooner if I kneel or squat, so I have to be careful, too, in the garden. Stand too fast after cutting in a little compost, and it's like my foot's asleep, except it's *me* asleep, all of me, not just my foot. Don't get me wrong: this is just a report, I'm not complaining. I'm alert to how little trouble I've had, compared to others. Still, there was a time when I didn't have to *think* about my each movement, the way I have to now. [...first.]

[First...]   In every other way not, so don't take the comparison wrong, but in this one way my studio on a winter morning before dawn, when it's cold out and dark, resembles a prison or monastery cell: confinement conduces to compiling percepts, noticing detail. I'm not nature's patient, sleepless Eremite, but in those early mornings I do *feel* like I'm watching with eternal lids apart, alert to pure ablution.   [...constellation.]

[Constellations:...]   I don't know what to make of the echo decaying from *spindrift* to *spendthrift,* but that doesn't prevent my being bent here toward answering the "wide spindrift gaze toward paradise."   [...disperse?]

[Dispersals...]   To reiterate: this isn't ordered into narrative, doesn't report the story of my life, just lists instance after instance of "infinite consanguinity." Let come what griefs and sufferings may, each one grace given gave all grace. Any one grace grace enough: enough to hear, against windless quiet and breathtaking cold, those tiny brittle sunstrucks settle.   [...sunlight.]

[Some light...]   This pattern, too, the reader many observe throughout. I attend to what might be called (by analogy with objective correlatives) proportional correlatives: commensurables linked across octaves or orders of magnitude. The innermost matryoshka doll and its outermost, the sixth-string E \and its sympathy-stirred sister first-string E. To note and number them not for curiosities, but for cues, as Socrates, spoken to by law, listened for Law. [...windowpane.]

[Pain...]   Actually only part of the house stands on slab. The older, original part stands over a stone-walled, stone-floored cellar, built before backhoes, back when people weren't so tall, so it holds the water heater, but it's too shallow to allow me to stand up straight. Another irony of decay: this stone foundation *composed* of fragments, not the slab, slowly decomposing *into* fragments, is of the two the more stable and secure.   [...one intimation.]

[One intimacy...]   It's true that the tent-of-dragonflies dream followed, and must have been part of processing, the experience of the whiteout, but the affect attending it was altogether other, the whiteout's enforced fear replaced in the dream by an equal and opposite calm.   [...less.]

[Less...]   They weren't kidding about the Manpower part of the name. The white male President created the Commission, and appointed as commissioners only white males. A few men, to tell a lot of women whether and where and at what to work. A few whites, to tell a lot of Blacks. A few bankers, to tell a lot of boiler makers.   [...we testify to.]

[I testify not to...]   Instances of proportional correlatives are multiplied here because I find it difficult to *conceptualize* what I know I ought to understand. There's a lot of falling and fading, because, even more often than it is hard to *conceptualize* what I ought to understand, it is hard to *face* and *accept* it.   [...integrity.]

[Integrals...]   Here the reader need not recall, though I have sought to invoke, Herakleitos' "Carelessly swept dustpile, the most gorgeous order." For one alert, as Ho Skoteinos was, to the lurking and the looming of the larger

68

than itself, an observation is a cautionary.   [...sea glass...]

[I see glass...]   Those voices of those friends: I'm trying here not so much to report what they say as to record how they sound.   [...*one one one.*]

[One...]   As law enforcement agencies track "persons of interest," so in the present work I attend to "patterns of interest," and this is one: events (such as, here, a riot) that, though not themselves within a person's immediate experience (such as, here, that of the boy), have formative and lasting effects on that person's life. Persons of interest, patterns of interest, places of interest, principles of interest...   [...right?]

[Write...]   Who, alert to ways in which institutions negate the personhood and violate the bodies of humans, would not be ever in search of community created and sustained in forms that elude or contest or subvert institutional reach?   [...the better.]

[Better...]   Feel free to disregard these glosses if for you they do simplify but do not amplify the measures they modify. Simplify, amplify, from the same Indo-European root, *pl-, fold. Feel free to note or to ignore recurring pattern of interest: the dramatic tension between *Myself am hell* and *I gotta get outa here.*   [...self.]

[Self-definition...]   Each new *declaration* of the principle stands as yet another *demonstration* of the principle that I see all and only what my language shows me, and see it only as my language shows it me. The limits of my language really do mean the limits of my world, a fact that accounts equally for how capacious those limits are, and for how confining.　　　[...more?]

[*More...*]　　　Call it a perplexity of interest: part of something's proving hard to find and hard to figure is its *seeming* self-finding and self-figuring. Which creates two types of conflict: a first, between those satisfied with the seeming and those dissatisfied, and a second, between those to whom one purport seems self-finding and those to whom a contradictory purport seems self-finding. And motivates two (conflicting) ideals for conflict resolution: voluntary mutual acceptance of inconclusiveness in findings and figurings, versus enforcement on all of what to some seems self-found.　　　[...the more northerly than itself.]

[The more than itself...]　　　Another pattern of interest: translations of mode across medium. Here, aesthesibility across sensoria (one thing audible as another is visible), but elsewhere deficiency across ensemble (market harmed by insufficient regulation as individual is harmed by insufficient courage), and so on. I count it a *con*ceptual correlative to the *per*ceptual phenomenon of synaesthesia. I make it a principle to match a principle here with a principle there. I suspect that principles sing to one another, and I'm trying to hear those songs. I suppose that the application of any one principle depends on the prior application of many other principles, with no ultimate principle, no unprincipled principle, to found and stabilize the rest.　　　[...at rest.]

[Addressed...]　　　Or, alternatively: Guess which hand. Guess which card. Guess which door hides the lady and which the tiger. Guess who sent the unsigned note. Guess I'll be going now. Guess who's coming to dinner. Guess what followed me home. Guess what I'm not telling you, and why I have to hold it back. Guess what I'm thinking. Guess what I heard, from whom. Guess I *have* to give it one more try. Guess what will happen if you get this wrong. Guess I'll go ahead and administer another 450-volt shock to the learner, since the experimenter assures me that "there is no permanent tissue damage." Guess what even your guessing right can't prevent. Guess again. [...eye.]

[I...]   As for my principle of activism, I have embraced, and offer the present work as one attempt to live up to, the principle (widely undervalued, most often offered glibly) *Don't just do something; stand there.* [...*how much.*]

[*How much...*]   It's easier to recognize an entailment relation than to discern a causal relation. Count that among the many reasons I can more often *tell* what's coming than *prevent* it.   [...another.]

[Another...]   I once knew a woman (though I didn't know her well enough then to remember her name now) who, with three of her high-school class-mates, had pledged after their graduation ceremony to sustain their friendship by convening at least once a month for the rest of their lives. Surely many sim-ilar commencement-day vows get made, but these friends *kept* theirs. When I knew her, they hadn't missed a month in more than fifty years. Even then, though, one of the four was ill enough that they had to meet each month at her home, and it's been so long since I knew the one that by now all four must be gone.   [...ice.]

[Ice...]   At the time I wouldn't have thought of it in terms of messages (I wouldn't have *thought* of it at all), but the impulse was strong in my childhood to hold my hand out the window when the station wagon was at highway speed, to hear and feel the wind. Of course my mother cautioned me to keep my arm inside, but who knows what she thought might happen, and who knows what I might understand better now if I'd been a little less obedient then.   [...pretends.]

[Pretense...]   I'd like to see the mask of Agamemnon, sure, but as for my own death I'm less concerned to have a mask made than urgent to be given an ushabti box to bear. Not stocked with servants to do my work for me, but with teachers to help me understand. Never mind remembrances of my fugitive presence; give me answerers for my ultimate absence.   [...axis.]

[Access...]   Another instance of the deficiency-across-ensemble pattern of interest: in proportion as I myself grow ever less substantial, my confines grow narrower.   [...know.]

[No...]   No further information is available at this time.   [...per serving.]

[Persevering...]   Maybe it's *because* so few familiar garden flowers grow at this latitude and elevation that I no longer see at all the butterflies I once saw often: monarchs and yellow swallowtails. (And, similarly, luna moths.) I miss them, but it isn't a disaster.   [...beneath their bodies.]

[Beneath our bodies,...]   A poetics: refuse euphemism.   [...during.]

[*During*...]   Think of this work in its entirety as testing the hypothesis (or as making a principle out of the fact) that only one aspect of loss can be seen at a time: now the duck, now the rabbit. Now recto, now verso. Now in flight, now at rest.   [...other.]

[Other...]   To the list above (persons of interest, patterns of interest, and so on) may be added paradoxes of interest. The reader is welcome to think of them as a distinct category, or as a subset of patterns. Though it may be an *instance* of paradox that I can know how you think of them more securely than I know how I think of them. A whole cloud of narrative condensed into one drop of lyric.   [...not in the least.]

[Not least...]   I'm doing all this counting, not to arrive at some final tally but to enhance my sense of scale; all this listing of luminosities, not to produce an exhaustive catalog but to achieve and sustain a requisite awe. In dreams begin responsibilities, in wonder begins philosophy, in truth begins reconciliation, in coruscation begins...   [...first.]

Silt

[If they were more wary…] This concern for distance is not peculiar to me, not a function of my misanthropy or my debilitating agoraphobia. All sociability depends at least as much on distance as on proximity. Except when they're forced into bait balls by dolphins or bluefin, herring maintain their group by each individual keeping its distance from every other. Starlings stipple a power line by settling each just far enough from the next not to be pecked by it. I'm not trying to draw you closer to me, my love, and I'm not trying to draw closer to you: I'm trying to establish and maintain enough distance.

[We had to climb into the trees…] All the adaptations that enabled the climbing up (independent movement of limbs, arms less tightly paired than, say, birds' wings) aided the climbing down, but not everything that helped us cope with canopy then furthers our negotiating grassland now. My eyes, for instance, would enable me to pick out the sharp outline of a limb close enough for me to leap to and thick enough to land on, but would not enable me to detect the stealthy approach of a camouflaged predator at distance enough to give me a headstart sufficient for escape. If other individuals had been more like me, the species would have gone extinct long ago.

[Such unsatisfying answers they evoke…] How long until this last short stretch of brick street in town gets paved over? What *will* the world be, once bereft? I know to close doors to the other rooms and leave the front door open, but how did that bird get *in* the house? How can we know the Griefgiver from the grief given? Would I be washed ashore or carried out to sea, or would I simply sink? Why *does* a perfect fifth sound so much sweeter than an augmented fourth?

74

Now what?

[Ice, necessity's best assistant...] Ice has the self-possession and patience proper to changers of state. *As* ice, yes, pingo and erratics and frost shattering, granite face fractured down to morain. But then, come spring or Chicxulub or the anthropocene, icemelt takes its turn, backing up waterfalls, carving canyons, beckoning salmonspawn, silting deltas.

[*I try to keep my interiority interior*...] I'd have to know whether I'm in the woods or facing an archaic torso, to choose wisely between Descartes' advice to stay the course and Rilke's to revise my life. Such context-dependency makes it hard to distinguish interior from exterior, self from situation, motility from medium. Makes me think I ought to take the jellyfish for my totem.

[Now it *is* later...] All this time I've been pursuing the capital-letter versions of the qualities I admire (Wisdom, Justice, Attention, Care...), even though I've only ever seen those qualities performed in the homemade crust of a pecan pie, the shoveling of a second stretch of sidewalk. Now I'm thinking that in some of those qualities (modesty, for instance), maybe in all of them, the lower-case version *is* the capital-letter version.

[So as to evoke but not fulfill...] They do still make bias-ply tires, though only for "specialty" uses: trailers, motorcycles, vintage cars. There's no one around anymore who remembers how it felt to have to fight the wheel that way, or could recognize *that* highway hum, or has opened a trunk big enough to hold a full-size spare, or cross-rotated instead of rotating front-to-back. And not many who could explain why radials run cooler.

[Drainage ditch, really, but I was taught not to fuss…] My brother loved to tell a story about getting sucker-punched in a bar when he was on shore leave. I never understood why it counted as something to brag about, but no doubt there was plenty he found puzzling about me. The triangle-folded flag a pair of white gloves handed them was one of the things my parents kept after his funeral, but not one I kept after theirs.

[It's not hymns themselves for which I hanker…] I still see the ten commandments carved in stone in front of county courthouses, so I suspect they still make grade-school kids pledge allegiance. Though maybe nowadays emergency drills are different. When I was a kid, there was under the desk, lined along the hallway wall all head-tucked, and gathered in the cafeteria, though I can't remember which was for tornado, which for earthquake, which for the Soviets starting a nuclear war. Principals must make pupils practice some equally futile drill now for active shooter protocol.

[Changes how the airport feels.] It's surprising how little it diminishes the effect of the stained glass inside the chapel, to have that stone-proof steel mesh covering them outside. Light's like water that way, though: seeping, saturating. I've tried to weatherproof my door, but at a certain season, time of day, angle of the sun, it's outlined, crisp and bright. Sisters it with my kitchen faucet, which doesn't drip when it's turned off but does leak a little at the base when it's running.

[These late-night walks give me time…] I didn't used to *have* to worry, if I woke with a new pain, whether I would wake with it every day for the rest of my life. I didn't used to *know* to worry who I'm harming not by what I do but by who I am. I used to could substitute one worry for another. (That's how she'd say it, "used to could," often complemented by a double negative, as in "I used to could do a handstand, but not no more.") Now I layer them.

[**I'd keep tissues in the glovebox…**] Seems more significant, somehow, when the nickname is *longer*, not shorter, than the given name. The kid in my junior high, for instance, whose real name was James, but everyone called him Deputy Dawg. He'd been held back a year or two, so he was taller and stronger than anyone else, and he had a beard. He insisted on the nickname (which I suspect he'd assigned himself), to honor (that, I'm sure, is how he thought of it) how many things he'd done with how many girls. Or anyway bragged of having done. I trust any reader *not* in junior high to know to translate that "done with" into "done to."

[**I have no answer now…**] As with stories and words, so with questions: you're given certain ones by the people who raise you and the context in which you're raised, but if you want others you have to go out and *find* them. And figure out for yourself how to fit which words to which stories, which stories to which questions. I've been so overwhelmed by the finding part that I haven't gotten very far toward the fitting.

[**No face now does not propose some other.**] I should have thought to make a time-lapse video of the slowly melting plowpile of snow across the street. Set up a tripod and take one still every hour, say. Not so much for a reminder of the fungibility of beauty and ugliness, simplicity and complexity. More because how often do I think about, and how else could I witness, the way grit first gets spread across the snow before it sediments down into mud.

[I see the by and by, by the way...] Bracket out what you were taught in school, just go by what you *see* when you drive a few miles out of town on a clear night and lie down in a plowed field. Then the ancient idea makes perfect sense: the sky *is* an inverted bowl, the stars *are* holes in it, they *do* open onto a Brilliance beyond.

[Not thinking I can make myself fox-like...] Cold nights like this, the glass panel of the changeable-letter sign in front of the church across the street frosts over, so for a while in the morning you can see that it spells out something, but not read what it says. Which, for those of us who prefer reminders of mystery to moral admonishments, makes dawn the best time of day to see the sign.

[It's not always people I've known...] The hoodie and his head-hung posture as he shuffles past does make him faceless, grim-reaperly. My guess is he cooks or washes dishes, probably both, at one of the bars a few blocks off. He always passes in the same direction at the same time of morning, right around 4. Never looks up, always has the sweatshirt's sleeves pushed past his elbows, keeps his hands in the pockets of those baggy jeans. I'd know him by his walk if I saw him somewhere else, say the grocery store, dressed some other way, but I wouldn't know him by his face.

[What I've been calling late-night walks...] From this spot the street itself is straight all the way to the bridge just past the last building, but stand here at night, and the line of light is not at all straight. The poles are treated timber, not metal, so some must be warped one way, some another. Though it *looks* like whoever stood them tested vertical by eye instead of by level or plumb line, and was satisfied with the standard my Uncle Alton followed with a spit,

"Good enough for you and me and government work." Pronounced *gumm-munt*.

[**I don't need to be told what they entail…**] They're not black-and-white, the "negatives" that linger briefly when I close my eyes, but the colors are much more muted than in whatever I've been staring at. They fade quickly, and I can't call them back, even though for a good while I can remember them.

[**Numbers keep to themselves…**] Attic room. A friend let me stay there when I needed a place just for a week. Only had two windows, one at either end. I don't much remember the view out the front window onto the street, but one afternoon out the back window I watched two kids in the next yard over, taking turns measuring out a plot, heel to toe. A field for a game? The layout of an imagined house? They went inside before I could tell for sure. They didn't wear matching jackets, but they did have matching shoes.

[**It has a *sound*, the moonlight…**] I seldom think they fit, but I like to try them on, wear them around for a while. Rootwarp. Time Lapse Ice Crystal Cascade. Sedimentary School. Enigmatic Megafauna. Festcrawlin. You're Not *Listening*. Tugboat. *How* Lonely? *Chimney* Lonely.

[**No use now, but who could…**] Hardly matters what "they" you mean, mice in the walls, bats in the rafters, termites in the joists, lactobacilli souring the milk. Or, for that matter, what "we."

[**It's still one thing, just leathern…**] Are my larger moral failures accumulations of my smaller, or sources of them? The field filled with grass, blade upon blade, or the trunk from which the branches spread? Should I be mowing or felling, cutting down the larger problem by cutting down all the smaller, or taking down all the smaller by taking down the larger? Is it a large failure or a small one, that I have to ask?

[**Not when they speak to me...**] Populations of canids for proof. If I'm hearing foxes and coyotes, it is and I am; if dogs, not.

[**They're my signals, too, now...**] Even in that basement room, shared kitchen, shared bath, both upstairs, unfinished ceiling, not quite high enough to let me stand up straight but I couldn't afford anything that did, one bare bulb, knob-and-tube, the one window one hand high and two hands wide that looked out through dirt onto mud.

[**In other words a rescue attempt...**] The bad news is that even though right now you take for granted that you'll always be able to, in fact you won't for much longer. The good news is that by then it won't matter as much to you that you can't as it matters to you now that you can.

[**We'd been bidden to bow our heads...**] Always the right shoe comes untied, never the left, though the laces are the same, and I double-knot them both. I *know* it's trivial, but because the pattern's so consistent even though there's no apparent cause, I can't keep myself from thinking it's *telling* me something. Which is made even sillier by the fact that anything it could be warning me of, I already know is bound to happen.

[**Not how things are supposed to happen...**] The obituary was nicely written, delicately leaving out the cause of death, which with matching delicacy I decline to name here. Though it makes no sense that we're all afraid to say what anyone who would care already knows, and what the omission itself tells anyone who didn't know. Any more than it makes sense that I didn't expect what I should have expected, and was surprised by what should not have surprised me. A lot of things that now I see were signs didn't seem like signs until afterward.

[Goes away no more than...] It's not the *quantity* that makes me want to give up, it's the *concentration.* I could manage this much pain if it were spread out, a steady flow instead of spikes, and diffused across my whole body instead of pointed at (into, through) certain spots. It makes sense that pain would happen where nerves gather, but that doesn't help. I try to imagine it spread out, I picture myself a self-immolating monk, the burning distributed evenly over my whole body, but of course that doesn't help, either.

[Not everything I say here is true.] She walked a step or two behind him. His shuffle was mechanical: head down, small steps, scooting his feet rather than lifting them, arms not swinging but held stiffly not quite at his side, as if he'd tried to put them in his front pants pockets and missed. His pace was steady but slow, very slow. She was talking on her phone. He followed the sidewalk. When they got to the street, she grabbed his shoulders and held him in place until one pickup stopped to let them cross. When they got across the street, she took his shoulders again and steered him, literally turning him so he faced east instead of north. She went back to her phone, and he followed *that* sidewalk until they were out of my sight.

[Foxes move when their prey moves...] Like the valley after sunrise but before

81

the fog burns off. Like this reciprocity: the quality light lends the fog, the quality fog lends the light. Like the way it transforms my sight into watching, my hearing into listening.

[The plane wasn't going to wait for the bus...] I didn't expect this cancer because I didn't know to expect it, didn't expect it *there* because I didn't expect it at all. Maybe I *would* have a family history of cancer if I didn't have a family history of beat you to it: head-on while intoxicated, not really a noose but it'll work, that much in your system and your body just forgets to breathe, in the tub as a kindness to whoever has to clean up after.

[Never been so close before.] I know the ringing is just in my ears, but it *sounds* like it's coming from somewhere far away.

[Who am I to criticize, though...] As species can share a progenitor without looking much alike, so words can be *closely related* without being *similar in meaning*. *Compliant,* say, and *complicit.* Or *repairs* as compared to *reparations.*

[The point is not this one incapacity...] I would have been failing even had I not known so, had I not felt my failure so thoracically, so loinfully. I will have been failing throughout the intervening period, if at any point between now and my vanishment into ultimacy you should check back. I had been failing for a long time before I could admit it to myself. I have been failing all along. I had failed fully as soon as I failed in part. I will have failed finally before next I fail momently.

[Have your papers ready.] Failsafe. Federated. Allied. There's a correspondence between facial expression and verbal expression, exploration of which is one thing I'm after here. *There,* for example: the expression "one thing I'm after." One thing I'm after is a registry of the effects of space-time curvature on one human life. One thing I'm after is a chronicle of disconfirmations. One thing I'm after is a map of undercurrents and counterflows and lag times. There's a correspondence, too, between a fixed expression and fixed tendencies. Of which I have many, including: to a see a world in an ice crystal and a heaven in a '67 4-4-2; to think the starving at the gate attest to, rather than predict, the ruin of the state; to link my recent emergence into one night with my imminent perishing into another.

[**One hand holds the other wrist as he listens…**] During which things fell apart. During which more war than peace, by far. During which names have been changed to protect. During which the surgeon general. During which occasional gestures toward civil rights, but no actual changes of place between gesturing and gestured-to. During which tooth decay, root rot, onychomycosis. During which my cold, dead hands. During which your regularly scheduled programming will resume shortly. During which unsubscribe.

[**Not for a single major failure…**] They're roofing the historic building downtown, and the logos printed on the tyvek sheets they'll shingle over make a grid across the main pitched portion of the roof, but half-cover one another in the awkward spiral that wraps the conical corner ornaments.

[**In this erasure, who is most erased?**] She thinks I should clean the windows more often, and I think I should clean the gutters tomorrow. She thinks the car sounds wrong when it idles, and I think it sounds wrong at highway speed.

She thinks we'll soon be forced to retreat underground, and I think retreat to the hills. She thinks docile and omnipotent at its own stable door, and I think keeps a rollin' on down to San Antone. She thinks there's more to this problem than meets the eye, and I think there's more than anybody counted on. She thinks straight eight, I think slant six. She thinks this is the time of year when almost every night, and I think past or passing or to come. She thinks the snow geese migrating, and I think the sandhill cranes.

[Maybe it means some underneath of me...] Not worried what to do for food once the grid goes down, just worried what to do when hungry, suddenly gridless people start passing through his parcel. Not afraid to die alone in the cold out in the woods someday, but afraid to die in a bed with siderails, hooked up to some machine.

[I'm not *so* incurious that I haven't tried to learn.] It's not like a hunter stalking prey through woods. Still, there's a trail of footprints, very faint but visible. It's across the one stretch of smooth stone, a kind of patio, that replaces cement for the width of one storefront. From their size and pattern, I'm guessing a man's boots. This precipitation (light mist, or heavy fog? is there a difference?) is just enough to make a medium of wet grit to record the prints, not enough to wash them away. I'm not following him, except accidentally, but they alert me that somebody else is out at this hour, assure me that somebody's already gone the way I'm going.

[Seems like I keep myself most often scarce.] Same with the window screen. Or similar. I don't notice it during the day, but early morning like this, more light inside than out, my glasses off because I'm at the desk working up close, when I look up, look out the window, the screen makes the streetlights into so many "Exit full screen" icons, makes an interference pattern with the shiny grid of corner-worn paving bricks on the wet street.

[**I know no proper name for either…**] Caution: this vehicle makes wide right turns. Trucks entering highway. Stay back 200 feet: not responsible for broken windshields. Oversize load. Protected by Smith & Wesson. If you can't see my mirrors, I can't see you.

[**I find no consolation in the consolations I'm offered.**] I know it's not the time frame of glaciers coming and going, tectonic plates testing one another, continents merging and drifting apart, but it was a *long* time ago, that year living in a studio apartment in a converted motel, listening to the voice-student across-the-hall neighbor, whose name I knew only from the row of mailboxes, sing scales. I remember it as three octaves up and down once in every key, every day the same order, start with C major, end in B minor. But I don't have the musical background to know, or the ear to tell, and it's been so long that probably I've made up much more than I've remembered.

[**I'd propose an amendment…**] Not that I feel *guilty* about anything I've done, just *embarrassed*. And that, because the lamentable thing is less the deeds done than the me who did them. It's easy to build out a good long list of people I owe reparations *to*, but since what I owe reparations *for* is who I was, it's hard to figure what those reparations could look like. More embarrassed than guilty about this, too: I have no reason to think my situation has, much less that I myself have, improved.

[I don't, but not from modesty…] You'd think all the fake stuff they make now, fake stone countertops, fake wood flooring, would secure the reality of real stuff, real granite, real hardwood, but it only makes the real as fake as the fake.

[They pass some judgment on my life…] Had to thin things out near the house: dead branches, dying trees. Too much danger of too much damage, if anything fell, and something was sure to fall. Less cover, though, cuts way down on the number and variety of birds that brave the feeder. The big aggressive ones still visit, the flicker and the jays, but not the tiny and timid. Been a while since I've seen a kinglet.

[Might should take my car in, find out…] Some irregularities, asymmetries, blemishes I've had from birth, others showed up later. Now, though, it's not just that new ones appear with increasing frequency, but that all the old ones get worse and worse. Whatever is mole-marred, crooked, who knows how.

[One eye wanders when I get a little tired…] Difficulty telling figure from ground. Difficulty making new memories. Difficulty keeping old friends. Difficulty breaking bad habits. Difficulty sleeping through the night, difficulty staying awake through the day. Difficulty expressing emotions, difficulty controlling emotions. Difficulty sticking to a budget, difficulty sticking to a schedule, difficulty sticking to a diet. Difficulty with airplane travel. Difficulty planning ahead, difficulty adjusting to change. Difficulty identifying even very common bird songs. Difficulty with small talk, difficulty with Hollywood films. Difficulty maintaining hope through winters this long and dark and bitterly cold.

[Sometimes the floaters rise slowly…] One more thing about the roofing of that historic building. The pitch is steep, so the workers are roped on, like they're rappeling. (No helmets, though.) One stays at the roof peak with a stack of shingles, two work slowly up the pitch. The one up top slides shingles down, like dealing cards, one at a time, to the others, and each catches his shingle, sets it, skims the air hammer over it, whapwhapwhapwhapwhap, even as the next shingle has started sliding down from above.

About the Author

H. L. Hix's other recent books include a novel, *The Death of H. L. Hix;* an edition and translation of *The Gospel* that merges canonical with noncanonical sources in a single narrative, and refers to God and Jesus without assigning them gender; a poetry collection, *How It Is That We;* an edition, with Julie Kane, of selected poems by contemporary Lithuanian poet Tautvyda Marcinkevičiūtė, called *Terribly In Love;* an essay collection, *Demonstrategy;* and an anthology of "poets and poetries, talking back," *Counterclaims.* He has been a Fulbright Distinguished Lecturer at Yonsei University in Seoul, and his *Chromatic* was a finalist for the National Book Award in poetry. He professes philosophy and creative writing at a university in "one of those square states."